Routledge Revivals

Craftsman and Quaker

First published in 1959, *Craftsman and Quaker* is the story of one man's life told against a background of the profound social changes of eighty years. Leslie Baily, well-known for his 'Scrapbook' and other historical radio programmes, extracted material from his father's diaries and letters and presented it as a very human story through this book.

James T. Baily began life in humble circumstances in Sheffield, where his own father was a carpenter and joiner. Through many changes of circumstances, J.T.B. became a teacher of crafts and in due course was recognized as one of Britain's leading authorities on crafts-teaching in schools, serving on a deputation to America to study methods over there. His methods and principles were far ahead of his time. During the First World War, J.T.B. organized work for the idle prisoners in internment camps and did similar work in Ireland during the civil war there. He also worked in Germany on famine relief. In the Second War, he had some remarkable experiences among evacuees and refugees.

A former secretary of the National Union of Manual Training Teachers and a Fellow of the College of Handicraft, he was crafts master of the famous Quaker school at Ackworth, a 'Mr. Chips' of real life.

Craftsman and Quaker
The Story of James T. Baily 1876–1957

Leslie Baily

First published in 1959
by George Allen & Unwin Ltd

This edition first published in 2024 by Routledge
4 Park Square, Milton Park, Abingdon, Oxon, OX14 4RN

and by Routledge
605 Third Avenue, New York, NY 10017

Routledge is an imprint of the Taylor & Francis Group, an informa business

© George Allen & Unwin Ltd 1959

All rights reserved. No part of this book may be reprinted or reproduced or utilised in any form or by any electronic, mechanical, or other means, now known or hereafter invented, including photocopying and recording, or in any information storage or retrieval system, without permission in writing from the publishers.

Publisher's Note
The publisher has gone to great lengths to ensure the quality of this reprint but points out that some imperfections in the original copies may be apparent.

Disclaimer
The publisher has made every effort to trace copyright holders and welcomes correspondence from those they have been unable to contact.

A Library of Congress record exists under LCCN: 59003169

ISBN: 978-1-032-86122-7 (hbk)
ISBN: 978-1-003-52142-6 (ebk)
ISBN: 978-1-032-86126-5 (pbk)

Book DOI 10.4324/9781003521426

1

J. T. B. at his bench at home, after his retirement. The plane on the bench was used by his father and grandfather

CRAFTSMAN AND QUAKER

The Story of James T. Baily
1876 - 1957

BY LESLIE BAILY

Ruskin House
GEORGE ALLEN & UNWIN LTD
MUSEUM STREET LONDON

First published in Great Britain in 1959

This book is copyright under the Berne Convention. Apart from any fair dealing for the purpose of private study, research, criticism or review, as permitted under the Copyright Act, 1956, no portion may be reproduced by any process without written permission. Enquiry should be made to the publisher.

© *George Allen & Unwin Ltd 1959*

*Printed in Great Britain
in 12 pt. Perpetua type
by Purnell and Sons Ltd
Paulton (Somerset) and London*

FOREWORD

In writing the *Scrapbook* programmes for the B.B.C. I have had the job of picturing in radio-pageantry the broad march of events through the profound changes, social, technological, cultural, and spiritual, of this century. This involves making some assessment of the influence of events on people. When we exclaim 'How life has changed!' we mean not only in material things like motor-cars but in the attitudes and responses of successive generations.

In this book, *Craftsman and Quaker*, I have had a rather different task, to measure the life of one man, instead of many, against the background of eighty years. He was my father, James T. Baily. From his diaries and letters I have extracted this story of how an individual was influenced by these immense changes.

I am indebted to my brothers Jim and Kenneth for their help, and to W. R. Hughes for reading and criticizing the proofs.

L.B.

CONTENTS

FOREWORD		page 5
I	*The Sweet Smell of Sawdust*	9
II	*Children's Heads are Hollow*	18
III	*Pubs, Puritans, and Patriotism*	29
IV	*Cathedral City in the 'Nineties*	42
V	*The Broadening Quest*	54
VI	*From Brooklyn to Borstal*	74
VII	*The Red-and-Black Star*	86
VIII	*The Malignant City*	98
IX	*Mission of Peace*	108
X	*When Irish Eyes Aren't Smiling*	119
XI	*Mr Chips Finds His Home*	123
INDEX		142

ILLUSTRATIONS

1	J.T.B. at his bench at home	*frontispiece*
2	Bust of Lord Grimthorpe in St Albans Abbey *facing page*	24
	Wharncliffe Crags	
3	St Albans Grammar School, the Abbey Gateway	25
	The King Charles fireplace in the workshop	
4	Woodwork class fifty years ago	32
	J.T.B. and J. W. Riley at Niagara, 1907	
5	Christmas cards drawn and printed by prisoners of war	33
6	Knockaloe prisoner-of-war camp	48
7	The knitting department, Knockaloe Camp	49
	Basket making at Knockaloe Camp	
8	A New Year greeting card from Knockaloe, 1918	64
	Wildmann's improvised tools and work	
	Clock made at Knockaloe	
9	Food ticket for 'Quakerhilfe'	65
	Vases carved from marrow bone	
10	Furniture made by Germans at Knockaloe for use in French houses	80
	Quaker relief workers building houses in France, 1918	
11	Repatriation, 1919	81
12	Sibford School, Oxfordshire	96
13	The Quaker Star in Vienna, 1919	97
	Distributing 'Quaker' soup in Berlin	
14	Ackworth School, Yorkshire	112
	The Crafts Department	
15	The old gymnasium at Ackworth	113
	The metalwork shop into which it was transformed	
16	The Carclew experiment, 1939	136
	The Warden (J.T.B.) in his office	
	J.T.B. lectures on his Quaker relief work, 1940	

I

The Sweet Smell of Sawdust

Eighty years ago under the soot-laden sky of industrial Sheffield the shameless rows of back-to-back houses, defrauded of all beauty, bore false witness to the purpose of mankind.

Here dwelt 'the working class', reproducing themselves with an unbridled Victorian fecundity they could ill afford, while nearby factories and shunting yards clanged and laboured through the night, and the startled darkness leapt back from the glow of steel-rolling mills giving birth to the materials of an increasingly industralised civilization.

From a shed behind one of these grey streets the sound of a carpenter planing wood attracted children to the door, to the sweet smell of sawdust. Gleaming rows of tools hung behind the bench, and as he straightened up from his work Grandfather James Baily burst into song: 'Stay, lady, stay!—for pity's sake, and hear a poor lone orphan's cry' . . . The lugubrious ballad rolled out oddly from this happy man, whose characteristic action as he stood there at the bench was to run his hands lovingly over the piece of woodwork he had wrought, a table top, or a chair perhaps.

One day it was a coffin. A neighbour had died penniless in the workhouse infirmary. Grandfather Baily lifted the coffin on to a handcart, and called for his eldest son, James Thomas Baily, the subject of this memoir, to help push it to the workhouse.

'When the gates were opened the workhouse gatekeeper rebuked us for neglecting to have the coffin covered,' said J.T.B. in later years. 'My dad glanced proudly at the coffin. "Covered?" he retorted. "Why should it be covered? I'm glad for anyone to see it. They'll realize that for once a poor person is getting something good!" '

Craftsman and Quaker

Almost to the end of his long and varied life, which closed in 1957, James Thomas Baily used in his own workshop some of the tools from his father's bench at Sheffield. These were his most treasured possessions. Tools were more than tools to him—chisel and mallet, plane and saw, these were the instruments through which Man's creative faculty might exercise; they possessed therefore a divine quality, they were to be applied only to the best.

'My ancestors were craftsmen,' he wrote. 'My father, skilled as a cabinet-maker, was very jealous that a high standard should be maintained, refusing to lower it upon any consideration.'[1]

James T. Baily's own life was to lead him into experiences far removed from the environment of the carpentry shop of his boyhood, but one can trace in his adventures a persistent effort to apply the integrity of the Sheffield carpenter, his father, to wider and more testing spheres of life. Anyone who lived to his eightieth year in modern times must not only have seen great changes, but—unless he were a dolt—must have been severely shaken and tested by transformations, material, spiritual, and psychological, which have made these years the most revolutionary of all time.

Income tax was twopence in the £ in 1876, the year when James Thomas Baily was born at Sleaford in Lincolnshire. The new baby entered a world in which British power was on the ascendant. Prime Minister Disraeli had in the previous year purchased control of the Suez Canal; now he added to Queen Victoria's titles the glamorous and significant words 'Empress of India'. The British Army dressed in scarlet, and the navy was adding ironclads to the wooden walls left over from Nelson's day; war was remote and picturesque, the subject of energetic drawings done in the field by 'our correspondent' and reproduced smudgily in the illustrated papers some weeks later. The telegraph and the railway had quickened the pulse of the world, but there was still a tendency for news and men to travel at the time-honoured speed of the horse. In town and country the clatter of

---

[1] *A Crafts Anthology*, by James T. Baily (Cassell) 1953.

The Sweet Smell of Sawdust

hooves was the characteristic music of the street, and the Victorian home managed to struggle along without the aid of electronic devices. But, all unknown to an innocent public, the Revolutionaries were at work; in this same year, 1876, Alexander Graham Bell invented the telephone, and Nikolaus Otto the internal-combustion engine.

Of more evident importance to James Baily, the cabinet maker, as he nursed his new babe, was the fact that since 1870 education had become compulsory in Britain for all children up to the age of ten years. Boys and girls over ten were permitted to leave school if they attained a certain standard. With the State cosseting his education in this extravagant manner the newborn son might go far.

Mr Disraeli had said that Britain was divided into two nations, the rich and the poor; the Bailys certainly were not among the rich. But nor were they poor, in the degree that poverty was then judged.

The family home at Sleaford was neither opulent nor austere. Its garden sloped charmingly to the river Slea, and when the Bailys posed in a group on the lawn for perpetuation by the New Photography they arrayed themselves in the top-hats and frock-coats and crinolined dresses of the respectable lower-middle-class which was emerging between Disraeli's two nations. But though they wore their best black for the family portrait, the Bailys were not infected by a genteel delusion which has wrought havoc in our social and educational system, namely that the black-coated worker pushing a pen at a desk is necessarily superior to the hand-worker. Too many good craftsmen had adorned the family tree—joiners, cabinet-makers, boat-builders, shoemakers—to allow of such a heresy.

It was to the old home at Sleaford that James Baily, the twenty-eight-year-old joiner and cabinet-maker, had brought his bride Susannah to live for a year before he set up his own carpentry shop at Sheffield. Susannah was the daughter of a Suffolk shoemaker, and a proud-looking pair they were, the girl dark and comely, the young craftsman of over medium height, broad-shouldered, with a sandy beard and moustaches. They embarked upon marriage in high spirits, a tragic future mercifully hidden from them. James Thomas Baily was their first-born.

James Baily of Sleaford, the grandfather of the new child, was also a skilled worker in wood, as witness several pieces of his cabinet-making which are heirlooms in our family a century later. The frock-coats and crinolines which were the Sunday-best signs of a modest well-being at Sleaford had been made possible by an addition to the old man's wood-working income: the earnings of his wife, but as her vocation was that of schoolteacher this augmentation was strictly guaranteed to remain very modest indeed. During thirty years as headmistress of Alvey's School at Sleaford Mary Baily's pay rose to £30 a year.

This might have been a warning to J.T.B. in later years. 'High pay is not one of the rewards of the teaching profession,' he used to say, leaving one to guess what other reward he had found. 'I myself when first appointed a teacher in 1897 received £90 a year, and my peak at a grammar school in 1936 was £480.'

Mary Baily was the grand-daughter of a Dutch shipbuilder named Ouzmann who had come to England in the previous century, so the tradition of craftsmanship flowed into J.T.B.'s bloodstream from that side of the family also.

After a few months at the family home in 1876 James and Susannah Baily took their child and went away to set up in a small house in a narrow street in the Highfields district of Sheffield. Behind the house was the carpenter's shop, the bench, the tools, the sweet smell of sawdust—an environment that made a sharp impression on the boy from the moment he could walk among the shavings and watch his father at work.

Sheffield was a rapidly expanding metropolis of steel, the home of the famous 'Sheffield plate', a city of proud Yorkshire-folk, where slums and riches were close partners beneath the smoke and glare of the furnaces. Misfortunes showered upon James and Susannah Baily, and any hope of riches swiftly evaporated.

'One of my first memories,' said J.T.B., 'is of my father in bed

The Sweet Smell of Sawdust

after falling from a scaffold when roofing a villa at Netheredge. This came near to being fatal, and my grandmother Mary (Ouzmann) Baily was summoned to his bedside. She rushed over from Sleaford to see him, a dear old lady in voluminous black garments and a bonnet truly mid-Victorian in its severity. I remember her getting into a one-horsed Victoria carriage after bidding us a fond and rather sad goodbye, and so to Victoria Station to return to her home. I did not see her again. My father recovered sufficiently to be able to get a job at a joinery works at Heeley, but work was spasmodic, and he became subject to epileptic fits, due to the accident. My mother, too, became an invalid, and was to die before I, the eldest of four children, became eleven years of age. My youngest brother was sickly. Poverty became ever present; to procure the means to live was a constant strain. There was one dark period when the grocer sued my father in the County Court for debt, and Dad was compelled to place in pawn some of his finest tools, a set of four steel planes. Yet he could sing as he worked, was held in high esteem, was kindly and considerate of others and dearly loved his family, and at the end of the day's toil would be happy and contented in our midst. His religious convictions most certainly had a great influence upon his life.'

J.T.B. had a clear memory, and when he reminisced of his childhood he often had something to say which marked the extraordinary changes in the social scene in the past seventy years. Sanitation is an example. If a nation be judged by its lavatories, we have gone far. There was no water sanitation for the Baily household in the city of Sheffield: across the stone-flagged yard at the back stood an earth closet with an adjoining midden to receive household rubbish and ashes: 'At certain intervals late at night I heard as I lay in bed the rumbling of the night-soil carts of the Sheffield Corporation, and I crept to the window to look down on the men with their hurricane lamps and barrows, arriving to empty the middens. They would be gone away before early morning after scattering disinfectant about, but the yard and its exit would be very smelly until the tenants set to work with pails of water and whalebone brooms, giving the whole a thorough swilling down.'

Sheffield was not exceptional in its primitive hygiene; the germs of typhus went to work among all classes. The Prince of Wales (later Edward VII) was struck down in 1871 by typhoid fever contracted from the bad drains of a Yorkshire mansion; many towns discharged their sewers straight into open streams and rivers until this was stopped by Act of Parliament in 1876, and in the 'eighties a water-closet was still a luxury in town houses and a paradisial dream in the country.

The Yorkshire housewife is a tartar for cleanliness, so one may be sure that the 'swilling down' was exhaustive. It took place at back and front of the houses every Saturday morning: 'The stone doorsteps and window-sills were washed until spotless and the edges ornamented with rubbing stone, a soft yellowish lump sold at the little grocery shop on the corner, which was run by a crippled hunchback who wore a big white smock to cover his deformity,' wrote J.T.B. in the memoirs he compiled in his old age.

'I remember the Catch-'em-alive Man. Town life in the summer was prolific in swarms of flies, aggravated by the primitive sanitation. To combat this unpleasant menace came a man who walked along the streets wearing a threadbare frock coat and an old tall silk hat, and fastened round it a sheet of newspaper smeared all over with treacle, which became almost hidden from view by a mass of dead and struggling flies. Under his arm he carried a batch of unused treacled papers made from old newspapers, and his cry was "Catch-'em-alive! Catch-'em-alive!"

'There were boys of my acquaintance who manufactured their own private fly-traps from hollowed-out corks, with pins as bars. In these prisons the flies were kept alive. I took no part in this activity. I disliked the cruelty of it, even to flies.'

The people of the 'eighties had no radio. The cinema had not been invented. The music-hall was not considered respectable, nor, in the eyes of society's puritanical classes, was the theatre. Today, in an age constipated with entertainments, we may wonder how our fathers found relaxation. They were more

The Sweet Smell of Sawdust

easily satisfied than we are; a few simple pleasures went a long way. J.T.B. told of the joy and excitement with which children followed the perambulating one-man band as he walked the streets like the Pied Piper of Hamelin: 'He carried on his back a big bass drum which he beat with drumsticks secured to each of his elbows. On top of the drum was fixed a pair of cymbals which were clanged together by means of a cord connected to the performer's boot heel. His hands held a cornet or a flute to his mouth, and sometimes a pan's pipes was fixed to the front of his collar, accessible to his mouth.

'It was also the day of the German band. About four or five players of brass instruments would stand in the street performing pieces of band music with more or less efficiency, concluding by one of their number going from door to door with hat or box. The performers wore a colourful military type of uniform and were usually visitors from Germany.

'The English Mummers' plays, dating back to mediaeval times, were still acted in the streets of Sheffield by groups of lads on Christmas Day. One character clad in black and armed with a wooden sword played the part of Old Nick, another that of St George, another a doctor.

'It was a custom on Christmas morning to visit and be visited, and partake of spice loaf and cheese. A saying of that time was that a kiss without a squeeze was like eating cake without the cheese.'[1]

Such were typical relaxations of the working class at a time when working hours were long and often dreary. Woodworker James Baily was fortunate that his job was varied; despite illness and misfortune, he was doubly happy that it gave him the joy of personal creative effort, at a time when most of his neighbours were caught up in the robot-like routines of factories and offices.

Domestic life, too, could be hard and dreary. In J.T.B.'s boyhood there was no such thing as stainless steel—'So I had to clean the knives and forks once a week, laboriously, one-by-one, on a leather-covered board on which I sprinkled bath-brick.

---

[1] Better known variant: 'Apple tart without cheese is like a kiss without a squeeze'!

Craftsman and Quaker

'As the eldest child of the family, I had many household tasks to perform. Saturday morning had its routine, starting with a long row of boots to clean ready for Sunday. Most footwear was black, and the polish was a soft oily substance like a flattened sausage, wrapped in greaseproof paper and known as Berry's Blacking. Boots were much more common than shoes; women's and occasionally men's boots were buttoned; elastic-sided boots were also much in use. During my lifetime domestic toil has been robbed of some of its drudgery by the invention of labour-saving devices such as the vacuum-cleaner, soap powder, efficient water-heating stoves, and electric irons and cookers. In my boyhood everything was done by manual labour. Washday (Monday) meant giving a helping-hand with the dolly-tub and pegs, and turning the mangle, which reminds me of a ditty we used to whistle and sing:

> Cheer boys, cheer!
> My mother's got a mangle,
> Cheer boys, cheer!
> She turns it with a handle.

'It was my usual task on returning home from afternoon school on washday to turn the handle of the mangle while my mother put the clothes through the rollers and back again. How hopefully I watched the reduction of that pile of clothes!—and felt a little irked when some, in my mother's judgment, required passing through more than once, thereby postponing my getting out to play or to the fireside to read my library book.

'Wooden tubs like deep trays were common in those days for washing, scrubbing, and rinsing clothes. My father made ours. He made numbers of these tubs for customers, and I too during my apprenticeship later made them as a means of raising funds.

'I remember that when at work he always wore a clean white apron tied around the waist and reaching down to the ankles, and when going to and from a job it was neatly rolled up around the waist and the end tucked under the roll. This has gradually gone out of use in most joinery shops.'

The Sweet Smell of Sawdust

Perhaps it is a pity that distinctive costumes for various occupations have disappeared in this country since those days, to be replaced by long overalls, or boiler-suits, or by nothing special at all. It has robbed the everyday scene of some picturesqueness, and it may be symptomatic of the worker's declining pride in his job. One of the first things that J.T.B. learned from his father was that this kind of pride is a virtue. 'My father had two personal toolkits, one large and one smaller, both in dovetailed chests, beautifully made. Each tool was stamped with the owner's name. In those days tools were jealously cared for, all metal parts preserved from rust, and wood parts kept clean and rubbed with linseed oil.'

A joiner's kit of tools cost about £30 for an average beginner's set, a lot of money by Victorian values.

'On the termination of an employee's engagement, whether by the employer giving him the sack or otherwise, the joiner could claim two hours for grinding and sharpening his tools, which enabled him to commence another employment with tools in good order. This was known as "grinding time".

'Holidays-with-pay were unheard of. Most working-class people were so poor that they never had holidays. I can recollect only one occasion in the first ten years of my life when our family got away by train to the seaside. The journey from Sheffield to Cleethorpes was a tremendous adventure, but *not* comfortable. Third-class carriages had hard seats with plain painted-wood backs, oil lamps provided a dim lighting, and there was no heating in the carriages other than a metal hot water bottle about two feet long by a foot wide. A porter came along the platform with a barrow-load of these foot-warmers which he distributed in the compartments. Toilet provisions on the trains were unknown; when we pulled in to a station the passengers made a concerted rush across the platform.'

II

Children's Heads are Hollow

Had it not been for the brave and epoch-making Education Act brought in by Gladstone's administration in 1870 the illiteracy of the British people would have had disastrous consequences. By 1881, when J.T.B. went forth to school at the age of five, the Act had hardly begun to show results, but in fact a social revolution had begun. The Act had made elementary education compulsory, and the establishment of schools the business of the State. As Sir G. M. Trevelyan says in his *English Social History*, England obtained, 'better late than never, a system of universal education without which she must soon have fallen into the rear among modern nations'. For the masses it opened up a new world of interests and opportunities. Coming as it did at a time of expanding industry, and of increasing complexity in politics, it was to have a profound effect on the social structure of this nation during the ensuing fifty years—and it was almost exactly fifty years later that Britain's first Labour Government took office, the natural political consequence of democratic education.

By 1881 the Education Act had merely given a first generation of working-class pupils some knowledge of the three Rs. Little more than the three Rs could be attempted until sufficient teachers were trained, until buildings and equipment were improved, and until the techniques of teaching advanced beyond the simplest level. J.T.B. casts his memory back to his schooldays:

'The infants class at Alderson Road Church of England School, Sheffield, was accommodated on a stepped gallery at the end of a large bare room in which other classes were held. We had to "hold our tongues" except when answering questions or

Children's Heads are Hollow

repeating phrases parrot-fashion after the teacher. The average teacher knew nothing of child psychology; as the jingle went:

> Ram it in,
> Jam it in,
> Children's heads are hollow.

Much time was spent in memorising, usually the whole class repeating together after the teacher. It was a babel of noise, with other classes being taught in the same room. I have a dim recollection of some large wall-charts which were occasionally taken off the wall and hung from the blackboard easel. Some were in colours. I was for a time bewildered when I was told that a certain four-sided figure was called a "square", and was later instructed that the same shape on another chart was now called "red".

'We sat most of the time with arms folded, except when we used slates in wooden frames, with slate pencils to write with. It was no wonder that after a few days I took a dislike to this. I had been used to much freedom at home. One Monday morning I lingered at the school gates until all had entered, and I fell to the temptation to give school a miss. But I suddenly remembered the twopence school fee[1] clasped in my hand; what should I do with it? If I returned home with it in my possession it would betray my truancy. Then I spotted a water stop-tap in the pavement. I lifted the lid, dropped in the two pennies, shut it down and went off walking and playing about the streets; unfortunately I had little idea of the passing of time and I arrived home long before I was due. I do not recollect any punishment, beyond my dear mother and father talking to me about correct conduct, and I was back at school in the afternoon and never again played truant. When I went back to my stop-tap money-box I found that someone else had taken the tuppence.'

Spartan Victorian day-schools knew nothing of medical officers, school nurses, free milk, cheap meals, shower-baths, clinics, medical examinations and reports. The most that was done was an occasional order to 'show hands', but it wasn't the dirty

---

[1] School fees in elementary schools were not abolished until 1891.

Craftsman and Quaker

hands of his school-fellows that stuck in J.T.B.'s memory, it was their heads. 'I have seen boys in the desks before me with lice crawling along their necks and in their hair. They seemed to be unconscious of the infestation, whereas, blessed with a home where cleanliness was made a strict habit, I was horrified. Unfortunately it was almost impossible to escape taking lice and fleas home, and my mother carried out a daily elimination exercise with a small-tooth comb.

'There was almost always a foetid smell in the classrooms, arising from dirty bodies and clothes. A school mistress had occasion to send one little girl back home with a note to her mother requesting that Mary be given a good wash, as she could smell her; the mother sent Mary back with this note:

Miss Pertikler,
    I sends my Mary to school for you to learn her not to smell her.
                            Yours truly,
                            Mrs Jones.'

Like many other serious-thinking men of the artisan type, James Baily, the father of our schoolboy, was strongly influenced by the winds of nonconformity which were blowing through Britain. He switched from the Established Church to Congregationalism. In politics he followed the radical trend and became a Liberal. He believed in religious education but he objected strongly to the direct management of schools by the Church of England—in this he was in company with large numbers of dissenters and agnostics, and in sympathy with the new Board Schools established under the 1870 Act, for after a great controversy it had been decided that in the Board Schools religious teaching should be given by teachers, not by parsons, and that parents who objected even to this could withdraw their children from the Bible lessons. James Baily was not against Bible knowledge but he was against the religious Establishment, so his changing views resulted in his small son being transferred from the Church School to a new Board School at Lowfields. Here the

Children's Heads are Hollow

boy was happy and made good progress under Mr Maidment, a teacher whose methods were ahead of his time.

The orthodox Board School lessons were crudely elementary and unimaginative. Drawing was simply the copying of pictures or diagrams from cards to a larger size. 'Poetry' was achieved by the class reciting en masse two or three pieces during the year: J.T.B. never forgot 'The Wreck of the Hesperus', 'We are Seven', and 'The Village Blacksmith'. His handwriting was of the copper-plate variety inculcated at that school. But he remembered with gratitude Mr Maidment's less orthodox methods, and in later years as a teacher J.T.B. was to take a similarly practical and experimental line. Mr Maidment's rambles were a case in point.

'On Saturdays he took us on walks out of Sheffield to the moorlands and green valleys beyond. When we got on an eminence commanding a good view he would trace a map of the district with his stick on the sandy road, and point out the places we could see about us—a very practical method of teaching geography and local history. I have a vivid memory of our tramping along the old Roman Road by Eccleshall and of his telling us of the Roman occupation and getting us to impersonate Roman legionaries on the march as we plodded along homewards towards Sheffield.

'Sometimes after a long tramp into Derbyshire some of us were apt to lag from tiredness, so Mr Maidment divided us into Red Indians and Canadian Settlers. The former had to ambush the latter, a chase got going, and Mr Maidment saw to it that the direction of the charge was homewards.

'Walking in the country in those days was rather different from today. The roads were extremely dusty in summer and very muddy in winter. From a summer day's tramp one returned powdered with white dust. Instead of garages and petrol pumps there were stables by the wayside. A farmer would go bouncing by in his gig, a fine lady in a brougham, a two-horse wagonette carrying a load of sightseers. I remember seeing a few of the original boneshaker bicycles. The wheels were of wood with iron rims, and the machine was propelled along by paddling the feet on the ground.'

The generation that knew the pre-motoring age is rapidly dying out, taking with it memories of sights and sounds that have vanished from country roads and city streets. 'What excitement there was', J.T.B. would recall, 'as the brewer's dray thundered along!—the massive vehicle, *so well-constructed an example of the wheel-wright's craft*, the driver perched high above with reins and long-handled whip; he and his mate, magnificent brawny fellows with full beards, wearing on their heads knitted red wool caps with tassels on the top, and girt about their waists with ample aprons of leather. They were superb horsemen, controlling the finest heavy draught horses, well fed, well groomed, and carrying an efficient and often ornate set of harness with gleaming brass-work.'

I have italicised J.T.B.'s reference to the fine craftsmanship of the wheel-wright because it was so characteristic of him. Though he treasured his memories, he was not a sentimentalist for the so-called good old days—the present and the future were just as exciting, if not more so—and for many of the social changes of his lifetime he had no regrets, but one thing he stoutly lamented and resisted: the decline of craftsmanship. His life may be said to have been devoted to nurturing those standards of skill and pride in one's work which are becoming increasingly old-fashioned. Beyond that, he wrote down his memories for their amusement and novelty, not with any envy of days gone by. The era of horse-trams and gas-lighting was picturesque—or it looks so through the looking-glass of memory—but it was not necessarily the better for that.

'The trams were drawn by two horses,' J.T.B. recalled, 'but Sheffield is a very hilly town and on the steeper gradients a third horse was attached to the front. I often saw one of these "pull-up" horses waiting at the foot of an incline, ready to help the tram up. It was in charge of a lad who had just left school, and who would ride astride the horse on its return journey to pick up another tram. Then the lad would hook his horse on and jump

Children's Heads are Hollow

on the platform next the driver. How we envied the "pull-up" horse lads!

'Street lighting was by gas. It was a familiar sight at dusk to see the lamplighter trotting along with his pole. At its top was a burning spark; on reaching a lamp he thrust up the end of the pole, which turned the key and so ignited the gas. A familiar saying in those days was "running like a lamplighter".

'In our home the lighting was by paraffin lamps in the parlour and the kitchen; in the bedrooms we used wax candles. Gradually gas came into use, at first in the form of a naked bat-wing flame issuing from a small nipple burner near the wall; later came incandescent mantles.'

It is, then, in the yellow glow of oil-lighting that we see the home of J.T.B.'s childhood. In the spotless kitchen stands his mother, the tall, slender, and black-haired Susannah. She was a devoted wife and mother, but after the birth of her fifth child her health broke down and she fell victim to the disease which was then a dreaded killer in our towns and cities, tuberculosis. The doctor paid frequent visits, the patient's bedroom windows were firmly shut, as was then prescribed, and a long succession of bottles of Dr Congreve's Consumption Cure appeared on the sideboard. All of which had to be paid for.

The youngest child died. Susannah herself became weaker. There was no money to hire help, so she sat in a chair in the kitchen supervising as her first born, now ten years of age, learned to bake bread. Before he left for school in the morning J.T.B. made a batch of dough, which was left in an earthenware vessel before the fire to rise; on his way home at midday he called at a nearby bakery to collect tins which he filled with the dough, marking 'B' on their tops with a fork, and on his way to afternoon school he left the lot at the baker's. In the evening he called again, to carry home the delicious newly-baked loaves, leaving a few pence in payment for use of the baker's oven.

At thirty-seven years of age Susannah took finally to her bed. One Sunday evening her husband had gone to Abbeydale Congregational Church and the younger children were in bed. J.T.B.

writes: 'I was spending the evening with my mother in her bedroom. She was dressed very nicely, and there was a large fire burning in the grate, for it was a cold winter. My mother asked me to place her large family Bible on another chair next to her and I knelt by her; she opened it to the fly leaf and I saw that she had written something on the page. She told me the Bible was a present to me. She gave me good counsel and asked me to lead a good life. This heart to heart talk left a deep and lasting impression upon me. Not long after, one morning very early I heard my father go downstairs and make a cup of tea. He returned with it for mother, and then from the adjoining bedroom I heard his grief-stricken cry of anguish. My mother had passed on.'

The words inscribed on the flyleaf of the big, heavily-bound book, included these: 'I hope you will take care of this Bible for the sake of her who has given it you, and not only for that but for the good instruction you may learn from it of heavenly things, of the love of the Saviour to you and the good you may be to others around you. Let it be, my dear Boy, your guide through life.'

It was.

Susannah's passing meant that for several months the household was on short commons. James Baily the carpenter was just under forty when he was left with four young children. He was in indifferent health himself. Then Annie Winter arrived as housekeeper, a quiet girl in her early thirties. Like magic the domestic scene fell into good order, and the children fell in love with Miss Winter. So did James Baily. Within a year they were married. Meanwhile the eldest son had got a job as errand boy to Mr Marsh, a nearby greengrocer and baker. Mr Marsh paid a weekly wage of one shilling, for which J.T.B. was expected on Friday evening to distribute bread, carrying the loaves in a basket almost as big as himself, and on Saturday to start early by sweeping the shop and the living-room behind it, to do various household jobs for Mr Marsh, to pack orders and to deliver them all the day long. Free meals were thrown in, and occasionally a bag of fruit augmented the shilling.

2. *'An angel wearing side-whiskers'* . . . *the bust of Lord Grimthorpe in St. Albans Abbey*

Wharncliffe Crags, the scene of J. T. B.'s boyhood Sunday School excursions. (From John Taylor's 'Illustrated Guide to Sheffield 1879.')

3
St. Albans Grammar School. The Abbey gateway, now part of St. Albans School. In the top room at the right of the archway J. T. B. organised the first woodwork classes in this oldest of English public schools

The King Charles fireplace in the room which was transformed into a workshop

Children's Heads are Hollow

On the Saturday when he received his first shilling J.T.B. was walking home when he came to a full stop outside a hardware shop: in the window was a pink earthenware flower vase, price one shilling. For minutes the boy stood with his face pressed to the window, then he went in and spent his week's wages. He took the vase home and presented it to his stepmother. The economic needs of the family were forgotten in this gesture, but it was one to which Annie's warm heart responded, and from that moment to her death forty years later they were devoted to one another.

The job of errand boy to Mr Marsh was an eye-opener to J.T.B. As he lugged his basket through the dingy streets he realized that, hard as the Bailys' life might be, they were in clover compared with some of their neighbours. Once, when a smallpox epidemic raged in a slum area he had to visit, his stepmother insisted on his wearing round his neck as a prophylactic a little bag of camphor.

Disease and poverty and cruelty were on every side. We may think it incongruous, perhaps, that the errand-boy carried with him a collecting card of the London Missionary Society, issued by his Sunday School, for the benefit of the heathen overseas; but there were a handful of his customers who sympathetically gave a few pence a week to his card. When Mr Marsh heard of this he indignantly forbade the alms-gathering. J.T.B.'s father thereupon called on Mr Marsh and sternly withdrew his son's services. 'So ended my first excursion in the labour market.'

A halfpenny or a penny a week was all the average boy had for pocketmoney. The 'cow-heel, pigs-trotter, tripe and chitterling' shop in the London Road, with its well-scrubbed counter, was a favourite resort when an unexpected penny came his way, and he would ask the motherly woman across the counter for 'A penn'orth of tripe, please'. Sprinkled with salt and vinegar, this was eaten from a newspaper, in the same style as the fish-and-chips of a later generation (J.T.B. could remember no fish-and-chip shops at Sheffield in his boyhood). From another nearby shop the white-aproned muffin man sallied forth with a huge basket on his head, ringing his bell and crying 'Teacakes, oatcakes, pikelets, muffins!'

Many working-class homes brewed their own drinks from dandelions, nettles, horehound, ginger, and sarsaparilla, fermented with brewer's yeast. And—'there was a very nice dish we had at home called frummity, made of wheat set to stew overnight, then boiled in milk, thickened with flour, spiced and sweetened, with fruit added.

'As for ice cream, I wonder we didn't all get poisoned. The ice-cream man was usually an Italian, black haired and olive skinned—or at least he was dressed as one. He pushed his barrow through the streets, selling his ices at 1d or 2d in glass containers like large eggcups. When the glass was emptied the ice-cream man would dip it in a bucket of water and wipe it with a dirty towel slung over his shoulder.'

If working hours were long and living conditions drab, the people nevertheless knew how to enjoy themselves when they got half a chance. Shrove Tuesday was a day not merely for eating pancakes but when people of all ages went into the streets to compete in skipping. The peg-top and whip-top season then started, and mothers were expected to make butterscotch.

'Unless my memory plays me false, we usually had Christmas-card weather in the winter. In the yards we piled up a big mound of snow and hollowed it out like an Eskimo igloo, where we sat munching home-made Yorkshire parkin, biscuits, and butterscotch. For skating we could purchase, for a few pence, irons with both ends pointed and turned up at right angles, which we hammered into the soles and heels of our boots.

'Shuttlecock and battledore was a popular game. By modern ideas our games were absurdly simple. We played marbles and leapfrog a great deal. "Peggy" was a popular game, in which a short piece of wood tapered at each end was placed on the ground, one end was tapped with a stick to make it jump upwards, and then it was struck with the stick to send it flying as far as possible. "Knur and Spel" (bat, trap and ball) was a somewhat similar game.

Children's Heads are Hollow

'There were a number of ring games played, probably more by girls, but sometimes by girls and boys together. In one of these we stood in a circle, and one person in isolation in the centre was supposed to act the choosing of marriage partners while we all sang verses. The last verse went something like this:

> Now you're married you must obey,
> You must be true to all you say,
> You must be kind and very good
> And help your wife to chop the wood.

'Another ditty we sang was a parody on a negro pastor's conduct of a religious service:

> Dearly beloved brethren
>   Is it not a sin
> To eat the good potatoes
> Without peeling off their skin?
> For the skins feed the pigs,
>   And the pigs feed you;
> Dearly beloved brethren,
>   Is this not true?

'All the cricket I knew as a lad was played on makeshift pitches in the streets and parks. Games were *not* part of a Board School curriculum.'

Sport was not organized on anything like the nationwide scale of today. It was not regarded as having anything to do with the nation's fitness. It was hardly commercialized at all. The Saturday afternoon football fever of modern times, our high-tension cricket Test Matches, our greyhound racing with dummy hares —such things would have seemed maniac if people in the 'eighties could have looked into the future and foreseen them, while the spectacle of millions of people sitting in semi-darkness in their homes, peering at screens on which other people followed these pursuits at a distance, would have been a glimpse of the inexplicable.

There were a few sporting heroes, mostly amateurs such as

the legendary 'W.G.'. County cricket drew most of its talent from the leisured upper classes whose public schools taught the game as a fine art. The democratization of sport, its spread on an organized scale to all classes, was just beginning. Professionalism in football started around 1885. Soccer was finding popularity in industrial areas like Sheffield and Birmingham, and the Football League was founded in this period. There was as yet little hockey or tennis, except among the well-to-do, and not even much pleasure cycling. The safety bicycle was invented in the mid-'eighties, the pneumatic tyre not until 1888; thereafter came the great bicycling boom.

In the 'eighties, according to J.T.B.'s memory, fishing was the most popular working-man's recreation. 'Beside the rivers and canals around Sheffield I witnessed a great deal of enthusiasm for the very ancient sport of the (more or less) compleat angler. Trains left on Saturdays crowded with fishermen and their wives, and loaded with fishing tackle, baskets and hampers. Many fishermen stayed the entire week-end on the river-banks, spending the night at a nearby inn or cottage. I had the offer of an uncle's rod, and I made an effort two or three times but it was too slow a sport for me, and I was far too busy with other things concerning my immediate needs to be a faithful follower of Izaak Walton.'

III

Pubs, Puritans, and Patriotism

There was a bucolic Baily uncle who kept the Bull Inn at Bottesford in Nottinghamshire. Occasional summer outings to Uncle Fred's were highlights in J.T.B.'s boyhood in those days when life in rural England still had about it a hang-over element from the eighteenth century: a flavour of the squirearchy and the peasantry, of huge meals of roast beef washed down by flagons of home-brewed ale, a tempo of rustic living which took its pace from the horse and the manual labourer. All this was in acute contrast with the way of life in working-class industrial Sheffield.

Watching the reapers swinging their scythes in the harvest field, the boy felt himself sensitised to a whole range of fresh experiences in sight and smell and sound. Uncle Fred let him hold the reins when they drove in to Grantham Market, and the Bull Inn itself was a thrilling place to explore, with its rooms and stables unchanged from coaching days, and smelling alike of leather and horses.

In every village and country town the craftsmen were to be seen at work—the wheelwrights and saddlers, blacksmiths, tailors, thatchers, stone-masons—a richly endowed gallery of skilled and traditional crafts which excited the interest of the carpenter's son from Sheffield and broadened the love of craftsmanship he had inherited from his fathers.

His fathers might have been less happy about another broadening influence on the boy during his visits to Uncle Fred's. In the country, he found, people were less strait-laced, less inhibited than the townsfolk he knew. The puritanism of Queen Victoria's reign was especially rigid in nonconformist and town circles; the Bailys and their kind were strict in their morals, repressed in their sex-attitudes, plain-spoken, sensitive in their social consciousness—which led them in their humble but sincere way into all manner of 'good works'. There was puritanism round the parish pump too, but on the whole rural life was lived too near to Mother Earth for the rude facts of life to be covered up. Lustiness of speech and behaviour, when he saw it, shocked and troubled the sensitive adolescent from Sheffield, but it struck the blinkers from his eyes. It was the beginning of a toleration towards non-puritans which made him a good mixer in adult life, and this was of immense value to the work he did in a wider world. J.T.B. was never able to cast off his own puritanism, and possibly he had no desire to do so, but the ability to mix cheerfully and easily with unpuritanical people, a capacity the pure puritan so rarely possesses, was encouraged in early life by the delightful but disturbing visits to Uncle Fred's.

Some of J.T.B.'s memories of them had a melodramatic quality. One macabre night he joined Cousin Ted and a gang of rustics armed with long-lashed whips, and they entered the village church, in which bats were flying about, and tried to bring them down. The operation proved of greater danger to the lads than to the bats.

Then Uncle Fred came to a melodramatic and untimely end. J.T.B. was not down in the country at the time—it happened in the depth of winter—but the postman brought the news to Sheffield, and it was read to the children as an Awful Example. Uncle Fred had attended a rent audit and set off late at night to drive home through a snowstorm, fortifying himself with the Demon. Next morning he was found dead in a frozen ditch, under the overturned trap.

'It was this tragedy', said J.T.B., 'on top of other incidents, which led my father to forswear alcohol. Drunkenness was very much more common than nowadays. Like most working men, Dad had been accustomed to his glass of beer, but in the city we saw around us so much misery due to drink that he resolved to be a total abstainer. In this I felt bound to follow his example when I grew to manhood. Nowadays total abstinence is often

Pubs, Puritans, and Patriotism

alluded to as though it were a symptom of narrow-mindedness, but I'm sure that the firm line taken in this respect by the head of the family in many homes had a great deal to do with the virtual disappearance of the sordid and brutal scenes which were common in my boyhood.'

The puritan warp in the Victorian pattern of life was quaintly interwoven into a patriotic woof—or perhaps one should now say with the scarlet thread of jingoism, for it was not true patriotism. Like all small boys, J.T.B. sang the jingo chorus:

> We don't want to fight,
> But, by jingo, if we do,
> We've got the men, we've got the ships,
> We've got the money too....

and like all Britons, big and small, he was nurtured in the belief that the British were the ordained top-dogs of the world. This was a period of rampant imperialism, and of enterprising colonisation. Red patches were being vigorously applied to the map of the world. Living in isolation on an impregnable island, and yet possessing an unequalled record for world-wide adventuring, the British, with their unchallenged naval power, were natural top-doggers.

'It gave us, I am afraid, a certain disdain for foreigners,' J.T.B. said as he reflected on those dead days. 'I remember how the remark "He's a foreigner" was used in my boyhood as of someone inferior, or even sinister.' When one considers that this comment is from a man who became a determined internationalist and anti-jingo, one may realize what a personal adjustment was called for in J.T.B.'s lifetime. The shattering of jingoistic and puritanical shibboleths by the revolutionary events of the twentieth century put many of the Victorian-bred generation to a severe tug-of-war with themselves. In their youth they were surrounded by an atmosphere of complete national confidence and self-sufficiency. Jingoism had not yet been shaken by near-defeat in the South African War. Keir Hardie had not yet entered the House of Commons to speak against war as an evil that working

Craftsman and Quaker

people, above all, must abhor, and to throw down his republican gauntlet, challenging public comparison between the pomp surrounding the throne and the poverty depressing the working class. Lacking such a lead, the working people swallowed the mystique of a flag-wagging age; in the 'eighties it was jingoism that was the opiate of the people.

We see J.T.B. at eleven years of age marching through the streets of Sheffield with tens of thousands like him, each carrying his little Union Jack, and wearing his Jubilee medal, a drum-and-fife band ahead, a brass band behind, as the contingents marched to Norfolk Park to celebrate the Jubilee of Queen Victoria. 'For weeks we had rehearsed our songs, from "Three cheers for the Red, White and Blue" to "God Save the Queen". Now Mr Henry Coward conducted the massed choirs and bands with his long white baton. Afterwards we crowded into the marquees where huge open troughs were full of delicious lemonade. In the evening there were fireworks.'

Fifty years a queen! The old lady of Windsor had become a symbol of the national self-sufficiency. Moral rectitude crowned her brow. Puritanism and patriotism were her orb and sceptre. The monarchy was a totem-pole round which the people took part in a mumbo-jumbo that they understood about as much as pagan tribesmen understand the esoteric rites of their witch-doctors. It was the summit of a highly autocratic society, and the ordinary man comprehended but weakly his own economic and political rights within this society. But very soon the improvement in general education, and the arrival on the scene of a number of vigorous disturbers of the peace who attacked the *status quo*, began to make people think, and set in motion our modern social revolution.

One evening young J.T.B. stood on a street corner listening to the forthright Socialism of H. M. Hyndman, aristocrat turned agitator, founder of the Social Democratic Federation—'a tall man with frock coat and long beard, he made a deep impression on me'.

The impression he made was not comfortable. Hyndman was a red-blooded intellectual Socialist. He was a rebel in a hurry:

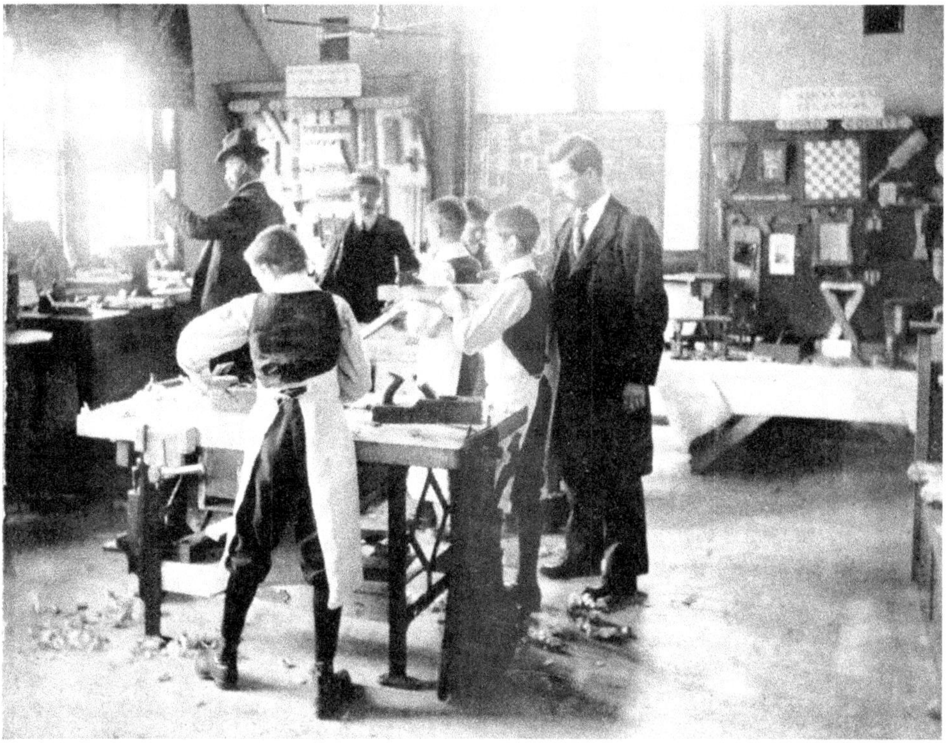

4

Fifty years ago: the woodwork teacher in frock coat is J. T. B.! The photograph was taken at a special demonstration of manual training at Croxley Green

The 'faked' picture of J. T. B. and J. W. Riley at Niagara, 1907

5 Christmas in captivity: as shown on a Christmas card drawn and printed by Germans at Knockaloe; and by British internees at Ruhleben, near Berlin in their camp magazine

Pubs, Puritans, and Patriotism

'I could not carry on,' he declared, 'unless I expected The Revolution at ten o'clock next Monday morning.'

Such sedition was regarded with horror not only by the aristocracy and the Establishment but by those respectable sections of the working-class itself over whom the patchwork blanket of puritanism, jingoism, and Liberalism smothered any tendency to violent kicking against a maladjusted social system. Bred in such an atmosphere, the boy Baily heard with disquiet the voice of Hyndman crying red revolution, and his awakening perceptions were still further assaulted by the fact that Sheffield provided a close-up of how maladjusted the system was, for this was the coming-of-age of steel. In ten years iron had been superseded by steel on the railways, in industry, in ship-building. Steel ships were only 10.3% of the tonnage launched in 1879, but ten years later they were 97.2%. A third of the world's ships were British, and our fleet was growing as we captured world trade. The Sheffield rolling mills thundered to feed the demand. Dozens of trades and hundreds of firms thrived on the boom in steel: engineering, chain-making, cutlery, tool makers, forgers, grinders, etc. Steel was wealth. The steel boom was Britain's goldrush. Yet the streets around the Baily home were dark with hardship. Furtively, the sweated industries hid from the light the wage-slaves in dark attics toiling for a few pennies a day.

Poverty crept into the Baily home itself. The craftsman in wood may not have been sweated as remorselessly as the chainmaker or the seamstress, but the only riches he had were the craftsman's pride and joy in the skill of his fingers. These are aesthetically rewarding but they can't be guaranteed to keep the wolf from the door.

As J.T.B. remembered: 'Sunday dinner at our house had its traditional roast beef, potatoes, and Yorkshire pudding, but on some occasions this menu had to be abandoned for bread and a tiny piece of cheese, my father trying to pass it off with pathetic flashes of humour such as "Now, a big bite of bread and a smell of the cheese, then a tiny nibble of cheese and another big bite of bread".

Craftsman and Quaker

'At all dinners we had pudding served first, a good helping so that we should not require much meat; if any of us protested that we did not want pudding my father said, "If you are not pudding hungry, you can't be meat hungry".

'We rarely ate butter. We had dripping which I fetched from the pork shop, and very good it was too. In our straitened circumstances we weren't miserable, but it was a struggle to live. This was worsened by a misfortune which befell my youngest brother Willie. He had seen a drunken man reeling about the streets. He came home comically imitating the drunkard, fell, and damaged his right elbow on the corner of the iron fireplace curb. This injury developed into tubercular disease of the elbow joint. Sickness in the home in those days meant heavy financial strain. Somehow, by hard toil, my parents managed to avoid our sliding across the last borderline of poverty into the corruption we could see in the slums nearby.'

The steel boom pushed the city into the surrounding countryside. When J.T.B. went off on school rambles or Sunday school excursions he noticed the long new rows of garish brick houses raping the green fields and sprawling up the hills with unplanned and ugly congestion; the aesthetic streak in the boy's character rebelled against this mean imitation of slumdom under God's good air. It was better than the back alleys and narrow courts of old Sheffield, but it was commercialism's tight-fisted guarantee that the new estates would be the slums of tomorrow. The boy, who was sensitive, noticed these things: 'Every summer we had a Sunday school excursion to some pleasant place in Derbyshire or Yorkshire, there to ramble and enjoy games and high tea before returning in the evening; these drives through beautiful country with lusty singing en route promoted an excellent social atmosphere; they helped to relieve the drabness of town life, but they also produced, in me at any rate, a healthy dissatisfaction with bad social conditions everywhere.

'In those days a bathroom was considered to be a luxury for upper-class houses. Saturday night was known as "tubbing night" when we bathed, from the youngest to the oldest, in

Pubs, Puritans, and Patriotism

front of the living-room fire, over which water was heated in a big saucepan and a large kettle, with a further supply in the side boiler of the Yorkshire range. The bath in our home was a wooden trough, made by my father. As I got older and privacy was required for bathing, I had to wait until all the family had retired to bed.'

The Sunday school at Sheffield had a room where boys could meet once a week for 'games, conversation, and reading'. This had a profound effect on J.T.B.'s questing mind. It began innocuously enough: *The Boy's Own Paper* and *Young England* were devoured between games of chess and draughts under the fatherly eye of the Sunday school superintendent. 'We could borrow the periodicals, and I remember taking home a copy of *Young England* and my father opened it after supper at a graphic narrative of the Charge of the Light Brigade at Balaclava in the Crimean War, which he read aloud to us with tremendous zest. Later I read the early issues of *The Wide World*, *The Strand Magazine*, *The Review of Reviews*, and *Pearson's Magazine*. My father was gradually collecting a little home library and he encouraged me to join the public library. I became a voracious reader of adventure, travel, and history. Reading became my best means of a continued education.'

The narrow walls of city life vanished as J.T.B. read how, all over the world, men were breaking their bonds—of new conquests in science, of new geographical discoveries. There was the new electric light. There was gold discovered on the Rand. The British Empire became 'wider still and wider'. A magnificent railway was built across Canada. The turbine was born. The telephone was a miracle. 'All these things thrilled me as a boy and filled most of us with a firm belief in the inevitable progress of the human race.'

From conquest over nature it was an easy step to politics and sociology, to reading about the revolt against the bondage that men imposed upon men, which more and more writers were fiercely denouncing. Hyndman had published *England for All* in 1881. In the years that followed, Bernard Shaw, Sidney Webb, William Morris, Edward Carpenter, Robert Blatchford and other propagandists wrote and tub-thumped, and J.T.B. read them all. He read, too, news of the unrest that was sweeping from industrial centre to industrial centre, of great strikes of match-girls and dockers in London, of the processions of protest against sweated labour, the police charges, the transformation of the trade unions from small bands of craftsmen banded together for professional purposes (the 'craft guilds') to powerful masses of workers bent on social-political reform.

'I count it my good fortune,' said J.T.B., 'that the years when I grew from childhood to manhood, were those of a great awakening of the British conscience. The mighty stirrings of opinion that then took place in the nation had a profound effect on my own thinking as I passed through the impressionable years of my teens.'

It was an exciting time to grow up, and an optimistic one, for even those who lived in depressed conditions began to believe in a Utopia at the end of the road. Yet in the respectable artisan class to which the Bailys belonged there was no hurry to follow the red flag. They mistrusted wild men. Traditionally they put their faith in the Liberals.

'In 1888 a group of men in Scotland, led by Keir Hardie, got together to form the first Labour Party, but it was long after that before the idea of direct Parliamentary representation for the working class was taken seriously in such circles as ours.'

This, then, was the tumultuous, changing England into which J.T.B. stepped on leaving school.

'To have passed Standard V at school and to have reached the age of twelve years made me eligible, in 1889, to leave for work. An advertisement in the local paper told me that a lad was wanted by Messrs Needham and Kugler, metal engravers, of Matilda Street. How pleased I was to be a full-time worker at five shillings a week! The engraving shop was a two-storied building at the back of a court of slummy tenements. My duties included fetching articles to be engraved, in a green baize sack, and returning them when finished, cleaning out the shops each morning and putting things tidy, and making tea. Each man

Pubs, Puritans, and Patriotism

brought his own bit of tea and sugar screwed up in a scrap of newspaper, and these I emptied into a row of mugs and made tea from a big black kettle. Water had to be fetched from a tap in the yard, known as "t'watter branch". My employers must have considered me to be a lad who promised better things, for one evening on returning home I found Mr Needham interviewing my parents and arranging for me to serve an apprenticeship to metal engraving. I commenced practising on odd pieces of metal. We worked a nine-hour day. After this I continued my education by attending evening continuation classes.'

Now came a disillusionment. Working alongside skilled engravers, J.T.B. was in a job where handwork still counted, though even here mechanical processes were creeping in; but as he went about in the workaday world he saw at close quarters the effect of the nineteenth century breakdown of craftsmanship under industrialism. His eyes were opened with a shock of startled discovery to the difference between his father's carpentry shop and the mills where multitudes worked.

He was disillusioned by the difference between their attitude to work and his father's. All through his childhood J.T.B. had been exposed, gently and naturally, to the conception that work is not done merely to earn a living, though Heaven knows the need for cash had often pressed hard. Without forcing his example down the boy's throat, James Baily the carpenter had been 'very jealous that a high standard should be maintained'. And that wasn't all. The ginger-whiskered craftsman who had been unashamed of the uncovered coffin at the workhouse funeral—'They'll realize that for once a poor person is getting something good'—was dedicated to his craft and to the service of others. In his humble way he was following the noble tradition of centuries of craftsmen whose mark is left indelibly on our land—on the village barn with its oaken roof marrying strength and beauty, in the cathedral where the same instinctive rightness of texture and form endures in stone through the changing years, in a hand-made chair, a wrought-iron gateway, a delicate embroidery, or a massive ship on the stocks, proudly blending the

Craftsman and Quaker

work of a thousand crafts, in all the masterpieces of the genius of English hands.

Through all the best of such work runs an instinct, the craftsman instinct, which you may see when first a child is given 'something to make', a skill which is far more than the good use of one's hands, for craftsmanship is related very directly to character, and through personal character to the service of others.

'Every rise in the quality of the work men do is followed, swiftly and inevitably, by a rise in the quality of the men who do it,' says L. P. Jacks. The converse is a truth that in the 1950s stares us uncomfortably in the face—that as the integrity of craftsmanship declines the stature of man shrinks with it.

In the 1880s these truths were the natural breath of life that the boy Baily breathed in his father's workshop, but when he went out to earn his living he was rudely shown that in modern mechanistic industry the dedicated values of the carpenter's shop did not apply. There were two main reasons for this. Mechanization tended to take individual craftsmanship and responsibility out of men's hands; and the conditions of squalid semi-slavery which some employers inflicted on their workpeople robbed human labour of all dignity. The serf can hardly be expected to be dedicated to anything but the forgetfulness of the gin-bottle.

Since then the increasing power of the trade unions has successfully tackled one of these evils—the exploitation of labour—but it is a tragic irony that the unions' immense growth in force and size has tended to amplify the other evil, lack of personal responsibility. Monolithic unionism seems to breed among some of its members a spirit of detached irresponsibility which denies the old-fashioned gospel that work equals service. J.T.B. saw, in his apprenticeship days, the ancient craft guilds superseded by the political trade unions, and he never ceased to regret it. He regarded as disastrous the disappearance of pure craftsmanship as a reason for workmen to band together, and one of the chief trends of his life was his attempt to redress this loss by introducing Craft Guilds in the schools where he taught. These were societies in which boys and girls were encouraged to put into

Pubs, Puritans, and Patriotism

craftsmanship, in wood, iron, or clay, in book-binding, weaving and basket-making, the same pride, skill, and team spirit that most schools see that they put into games. After his retirement J.T.B. was one of the founders of the Welwyn Crafts Guild, an adult society with the same purpose. Some of its members were professional wood and metal workers, weavers, etc., others were people of other occupations who found the crafts a spare-time outlet. So to the end of his life J.T.B. was a missionary of craftsmanship, and it all began when an impressionable youth was shocked by industrialism.

It was Uncle Joe who put him on the first step of the ladder that led from the obscurity of an engraver's workshop in Sheffield. Uncle Joe was a very different type from Uncle Fred, and he stepped into J.T.B.'s life at a time of crisis:

'My father died suddenly of pneumonia at forty-two years of age. My step-mother was left with four children, after only three years of married life. She was also left with a burden of debt through my father's misfortunes. The workshop, bench, lathe, and mortice machine, and a small stock of timber went to a timber merchant to defray the debt owing him. I found myself at thirteen and a half the breadwinner of the family. This was an impossible situation. The solution—and it was a painful one—was that my step-mother should remove to Lincoln to the home of her parents, taking my brothers Alfred and Willie with her. My sister Janie was received into an orphanage at Birmingham. I was to remain at Sheffield. I prepared to give up my evening classes and work all hours to make ends meet. Then came a message from my Uncle Joe to visit him at his office.'

J.T.B. walked round to the workshops where school desks and chairs were being repaired, for Joseph William Baily was Clerk of Works to the Sheffield School Board. The boy's ears pricked up as he heard the musical rasp of a saw. This was the atmosphere of his father's workshop again. How he loved the smell of sawdust, the sheen of newly-planed timber.

'What's happening about tha future, lad? . . . Giving up evening classes? Tha mustn't do owt o't'sort.'

Craftsman and Quaker

'But I haven't the money, Uncle . . .'

'I'll see to that. Giving up classes, a bright lad like you, Jim; it'd be criminal. How d'you like the engraver's shop?'

'It's all right.'

'Nowt like a woodwork shop, is there?'

'No, Uncle Joe. There isn't.'

So, under Uncle Joe's patronage, J.T.B. left the steel-engraver and was apprenticed to Mr Robinson, carpenter and builder; and the evening classes were resumed. 'I was much happier,' said J.T.B., 'in joinery than in engraving.' He was showing the same genius for woodwork as his father and grandfather before him.

One day Uncle Joe invited his nephew to drop in at the Sheffield Central School. J.T.B. had heard much talk of this, for it was a new name for a new type of school. He saw a classroom fitted up as a workshop, a thing he had never seen before—a thing which was unique in Britain. His own Board School had given J.T.B. no teaching at all in the use of his hands, apart from some very dull drawing lessons. He stood now enthralled, watching a class of boys at the benches, and thinking to himself (at fourteen!) how much better their education was than his had been.

Uncle Joe was a pioneer. This is what Professor Bennett, the historian of craft teaching, writes about him:[1]

Sheffield has been given the credit of being the first to organise what in England is called a Central School. This was a school made up of the brightest or specially talented pupils from the other elementary schools in the district. In the year 1880 the first school of this type was established. The science master was W. Ripper, later Professor Ripper, Head of the Technical Department, Sheffield University. In order to make his science instruction more interesting and more effective, he induced the School Board to fit up a shop for work in wood and iron, including in the equipment a lathe and a forge. The workshop

---

[1] *The History of Manual and Industrial Education* by Charles A. Bennett (Manual Arts Press, USA) 1926.

Pubs, Puritans, and Patriotism

instructor was Joseph William Baily, a skilled craftsman and Clerk of Works to the Sheffield School Board. He was the uncle of James T. Baily, Secretary of the National Association of Manual Training Teachers in 1908.

'So my Uncle Joe and I came into the same orbit of educational activity, though at different periods. In 1889, when he helped me to continue my education at evening classes, I never dreamt I should become a teacher, though, like most adolescents, I had my day-dreams of better things.'

IV

Cathedral City in the 'Nineties

Barges and other canal boats made a bright and busy traffic through the lock gates at Stamp End, in the valley below the memorable hill that is crowned by Lincoln cathedral, and every angler and every schoolboy knew how you could look in the still waters of the River Witham at a suitable angle and see, upside down, the triple towers of the wonderful building that dominates the city of Lincoln and all the country around.

When J.T.B., a teenager in long trousers and cloth cap, saw that reflected image and then turned his eyes to 'the noblest towers in Christendom' (as they have been called), on Lincoln's hill-top, he was making first contact with something his life had lacked, but which must be of significance to every craftsman and artist: a sense of tradition. School history at Sheffield had been a smattering of dates, kings, and battles. It had no apparent connection with present life; so it was a revelation to the lad now to see the work of Roman, Saxon, Norman, and Gothic hands passing down, through the thirteenth-century wrought-iron screens and the cathedral library designed by Wren, to the present day. Here was the labour of countless generations of foresters, woodworkers, carvers, quarrymen, masons, blacksmiths, builders, glass-makers, copper-smiths and silver-smiths; it blended in glorious harmony, as the sounds of a hundred musical instruments blend in a symphony, and as one tried to comprehend it one was conscious of some inner mystery, the power of faith and of beauty living in dead stone and timber that had been wrought by men who believed in something, and so gave to the inert a mystic and enduring life.

When watching his father working at some fine piece of

cabinet-making, J.T.B. had already glimpsed what perfection means. Now, as he climbed the hill to the cathedral, he saw it on a grand scale. 'I marvelled,' he said, 'at how perfect this perfection was.'

He came, in his reading, across a saying of Michelangelo's: 'God is Perfection, and whoever strives for perfection strives for something that is God-like.' He wrote it down in his notebook.

These things that shape a career may seem accidental, but they are only so in part. The puff of wind is accidental but the hand that swiftly pulls the sail to catch it is deliberate. The relationship of craftsmanship to perfection, and therefore to something God-like on earth, was a course to which J.T.B. tried to shape his course quite deliberately; but the revelation that came to him on Lincoln's hill was the result of an accident—the closing of Mr Robinson's business in Sheffield had put his apprentice, J.T.B., out of a job. And so he came to Lincoln.

The lock-keeper at Stamp End was John Winter, father of Annie, that same motherly Annie who had been so soon widowed after taking under her wing the carpenter's family at Sheffield, and who had come back here with two small step-children. She had missed the eldest Baily boy, and he had missed her, and when Mr Robinson's business collapsed J.T.B. was taken under John Winter's hospitable roof at The Lock House.

'When my step-mother asked me what I wanted to do I replied that I still wished to learn carpentry and joinery. I was apprenticed to a Lincoln firm of builders named Lansdown for seven years, starting at five shillings a week. I went off to my job carrying the excellent kit of tools left to me by my father. The new apprentice was always the victim of practical jokes, and I was no exception. I knew what it was to be sent to a neighbouring ironmonger's with an order for a dozen keyholes, or to be told to go to the workshop store and ask George for a drop of strap-oil. George, being a party to the joke, had a leather strap ready to apply to one's innocent behind. Another joke was to glue the victim's plane to the bench.

Craftsman and Quaker

'I found the work at Lansdown's very hard but interesting. We started at 6 a.m. and did a fifty-three-and-a-half-hour week. The firm had a big contract with the Midland Railway for repair work between Lincoln and Nottingham, and this I liked because it involved travelling to stations and gatehouses to do repairs and alterations. One of my jobs was the regular repair of the smoke-boards over the platform at Lincoln station. It was dirty work, frequently interrupted by the arrival of trains, and I went home looking like a chimney-sweep.

'I fitted up one of the outhouses at the Lock House as a private workshop so that in my spare time I could do odd jobs for relatives and others, making shelving and so on to earn a little money to buy tools and books. I was keen on the finer forms of woodwork—inlaying, cabinet-making, and the designing and execution of small highly finished work—which did not often come my way at Lansdown's, but there was little time for this as my step-mother wisely insisted that I went regularly to evening continuation classes. The curriculum was mathematics, English, technical drawing, physiography, and physical training, for which two army sergeants from Lincoln Barracks attended to put us through our paces. Their instruction was given under difficulties, as there was little available space and we simply stood up behind our desks. The drill was accompanied by the singing of such inappropriate songs as:

> Sailing, sailing, over the bounding main,
> There's many a stormy wind shall blow,
> Till Jack comes home again.

'After a full day's work at my trade, usually in the open air, to come to a stuffy classroom in the evening was hard going, and I often caught myself falling asleep at my desk. It really was too much, physically and mentally, for youngsters in their early teens. Nevertheless, I count it well worth the effort.

'Life wasn't all work. Opportunities for entertainment were rare, but they stand out the more vividly for that. Popular concerts were held in the Corn Exchange in the winter, and one of

Cathedral City in the 'Nineties

the greatest events was the visit of the Fisk Jubilee Singers, negroes from the USA who had been slaves, or children of slaves. They were the introducers of negro spirituals to this country, and very wonderful we thought their singing.

'An invitation to London to spend a holiday with some aunts, was a great adventure—to walk the crowded gas-lit streets, to ride on the horse-drawn buses with back-to-back seats on the top, like two garden seats placed lengthwise, to travel on the underground railway, then steam driven. Clouds of acrid smoke smothered carriages and stations with soot, and the atmosphere everywhere was pungent with sulphur. I preferred the horse-bus, despite the fact that in hot weather the city streets had an odour very different from the petrol fumes of today. I was astonished by the deftness with which the scavenging boys nipped between the vehicles and horses to sweep up the droppings.

'On Sunday morning in London I decided to attend the service at the City Temple to hear Dr Joseph Parker, one of the most famous preachers of the Congregational Church. My aunt's home was off the Harrow Road, so I had to start early to walk several miles along Harrow Road, Edgware Road, Oxford Street and Holborn to Holborn Viaduct. I arrived early, but the church was full. I do not recollect much about the sermon, but I do remember Dr Parker's patriarchal figure, and how, in condemning the Turkish atrocities in Armenia he cried indignantly, "God damn the Sultan".'

A young man who took the trouble to go to hear such a preacher, and who had an enquiring mind and a voracious appetite for reading, was certain to come up against spiritual problems and mental hazards, especially when he worked shoulder to shoulder with some rough characters, as the following story tells.

'One day our carter Sam was delivering a cartload of materials at a pair of villas we were building on West Parade. Just as we started dinner he gave the horse his nosebag and came to sit with us on the plank. Sam was an old soldier and the talk got round to his experiences during the Sudan War against the "fuzzy-wuzzies", as he called them. He described to us a battle in the

Craftsman and Quaker

desert, how before the dawn the scarlet-coated British troops were formed into a huge hollow square with bayonets fixed.

' "I tell you, lads", he said, "we all had the belly ache, especially when day came and we saw great hordes of yelling bloody savages rushing down upon us, brandishing their spears and yelling like hell. But then a wonderful thing happened. At the sound of the first shot from the British square everything changed, we seemed to lose all our fear, we became a mass of cursing, yelling madmen pouring in a withering fire, and when the onslaught of the fuzzy-wuzzies was spent, we up and charged the devils with cold steel. We fell upon 'em like murder and them as was left fled from us."

' "Did you get hurt, Sam?" asked one of my workmates.

'Sam's answer was to bare his abdomen, revealing a long scar on the right side:

' "A fuzzy got me with his spear", he said.'

The quiet little apprentice who sat on the plank listening to this savage tale couldn't get it out of his mind afterwards. He had been brought up in an atmosphere of peace, for the hardships of the Sheffield home had made no difference to the fact that the text framed on the wall was taken seriously: 'God is Love.' And although Susannah and James Baily had been reticent to their son over sex questions, they had at least conveyed to him the idea that the human body is a thing of perfection, to be respected, and to be treated, as they would say, as a gift from God. It seemed difficult to reconcile the gospels of love and of perfection with the lust and murder of Sam's anecdote. How could men, such genial homely men as Sam, act so to other men?—and invariably 'in a Christian cause', as it was officially asserted. How could 'God is Love' be equated to 'God damn the Sultan'?

The puzzled young man thought of 'the noblest towers in Christendom', up there on Lincoln's hill, and of how multitudes of men had toiled to make such perfection 'for the glory of God', and he couldn't understand how the leaders of the Church, who cherished such monuments in stone for the glory of the Creator, should fail to denounce the mutilation and annihilation of God's

Cathedral City in the 'Nineties

own most glorious creation, and should even bless the instruments of mutilation and death.

The questing mind of J.T.B. was perplexed as he tried to relate his upbringing to the realities of the world. He was off on that quest for truth and beauty and love which was to be his lot to the very end.

If religion perplexed him, so did politics. While still an apprentice the problem of capitalism suddenly presented itself in a way which, in later life, he related with a chuckle:

'I had obtained a private commission to make a piece of woodwork in my spare time and I asked a younger apprentice to help me at an agreed wage per hour. When we had completed the work and I had been paid I found that I had made a profit over and above the amount of the normal wages we had both earned. It was at this point that there came a challenge in my mind. I knew that it was usual for the employer to retain any profit left, but had not my assistant contributed equally with myself in accumulating that profit? What if our roles were reversed and he was the employer and I the employee, what then? "As ye would that men should do to you, do ye also to them likewise." I pondered upon what I regarded as a test of my Christian beliefs. At the same time I was attracted to the Socialistic issues promulgated by Keir Hardie and others, and I felt it would be a betrayal to harden my heart in the little matter of sharing the surplus profit with my mate; it was the same principle. So we shared it.'

Keir Hardie had by now made his famous debut in the House of Commons, in the tweed jacket and cloth cap that shocked the respectable; and the Independent Labour Party had been formed. In the 'nineties political and economic reform was burning with a bright light in Britain, and high was the pressure of pure idealism that fed its searing flame, so it was no wonder if such an idealistic youth as J.T.B. was tempted to leave his bench and throw in his lot with the reformers. But it was not political reform that nearly deprived Lansdown's of a promising apprentice. He suddenly decided he wanted to become a missionary. His reading about men like Livingstone had prepared his imagination, and when

Craftsman and Quaker

James Chalmers, a missionary home on leave from New Guinea, addressed a meeting at Lincoln, J.T.B. was convinced that his own life work lay among the cannibals of that island, or the heathen of Africa. He was not going to forsake his crafts altogether: 'The idea was that I should offer myself as an artisan missionary to train backward tribes in crafts and trades.'

J.T.B. took counsel of his 'spiritual father', as he called the Rev. J. D. Jones, the fervent Welshman who was at this time ministering in Lincoln and later became nationally nicknamed 'The Bishop of Congregationalism' when chairman of the Congregational Union of England and Wales. Mr Jones encouraged the young zealot, arranged for him to join a class for lay preachers, and introduced him to the London Missionary Society.

'I went to London for a medical examination. The verdict was that my own health was very good, with every promise of a long and useful life, but that my family medical history was such that I could not be accepted. On my return, disappointed, I reported the result to the Rev. Jones.

' "Well, James," he said, "that seems to be a closed door, but remember that when God closes one door He usually opens another." '

The medical history was indeed bad. Since J.T.B. had joined his step-mother at Lincoln she had lost two of her charges. Willie, the little boy with the crippled arm, died at twelve years of age, of tuberculosis. In the same year Janie returned from the orphanage and died at seventeen, also from TB.

'These bereavements affected me deeply, for I was affectionately attached to both sister and brother. It was natural, too, that fear of this disease should assail me, and should affect my emotions for some years, for it had previously carried off my mother, and in those days "consumption" was little understood by the medical profession. Treatment (such as it was) was in some respects the opposite of modern methods. Now that in old age I contemplate the vast strides of medical science and social hygiene, and the devoted and wonderful work of the medical

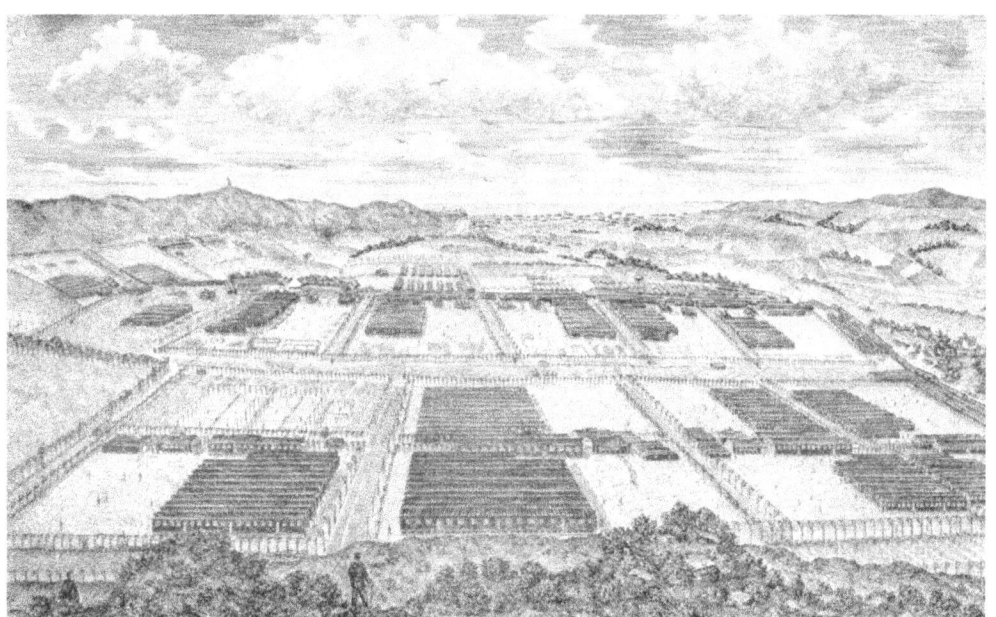

6

Knockaloe, Isle of Man: a steel engraving made in the camp. The view is looking westwards towards Peel and the sea

Wood engravings made in Knockaloe camp, by F. Nettel, an Austrian

The knitting department in Knockaloe camp, where three pairs of old socks were unwound and re-knitted into one new pair

ABOVE:
Basket making: a new Manx industry starts inside the barbed wire at Knockaloe camp

LEFT:
Basket-making at Knockaloe internment camp: Major Quayle-Dickson, commandant of Camp 3, with Edward Lewis, the Quaker relief representative, and J. T. Baily, the Industrial Superintendent, 1918

Cathedral City in the 'Nineties

profession, I feel like the sisters of Lazarus who said to Jesus, "Hadst thou been here, our brother had not died".

'Only my brother Alfred and I were left now. He too was to pass on at thirty years of age through lack of hospital accommodation and proper treatment, in the days before these were provided by the State.

'But remorse for the past is pointless. Remorse is replaced by rejoicing when I look around at my children and grandchildren and see what a better chance they have before them of full and healthy lives. My own life has been prolonged beyond the span of three score years and ten by methods that were unknown half a century ago.'

In 1880 the number of deaths caused by tuberculosis in England and Wales was 74,589. In 1957, out of a population which had doubled in the meantime, 4,784 died from this disease. This phenomenal drop is due not only to medical advance, but to the improvement in the living conditions of the people—housing, hygiene, schools, etc. After his rejection as a missionary, J.T.B. soon realized that social missionaries were needed in darkest England just as much as religious missionaries in darkest Africa, or more so.

As he went about Lincoln he found more and more to enjoy and to study in the old walls and gates of the city, the Stone Bow, the High Bridge with its houses built mediaeval-wise over the river, the Cathedral Close with Great Tom booming overhead. But Lincoln also had its industries and soon he was exploring its slums, not out of curiosity but because the Rev J. D. Jones's lamp was apt to penetrate into the darkest corners of society, and J.T.B. was among the bands of workers who manned the Congregational missions and chapels. He was growing to manhood now, a short sturdily-built fellow with dark hair, a gingerish moustache, a boisterous laugh, and a healthiness that conflicted amazingly with the dreadful family history. His vitality was exceptional. As a lay preacher, 'I was surprised to find myself doing all sorts of things from baptizing a baby to conducting the choir.'

Craftsman and Quaker

When Dr Jones wanted a new chapel extension J.T.B. promptly set to work, drew the plans, begged subscriptions, rounded up voluntary labour, and with the evening help of shop assistants and clerks under guttering oil-flares, built it, with himself (aged twenty) as foreman. It was characteristic of J.T.B. to find so practical an outlet for his idealism.

There was a slum called Ashton's Court where a mission was occasionally held under 'darkest England' conditions. The Court consisted of dilapidated tenements, overcrowded, insanitary, dirty, badly infested with fleas and bugs, beetles and lice, rats and mice. The occupants were poverty-stricken, drink-sodden, unclean, quarrelsome, and frequently figured in the police courts. It was a place avoided by most people. When two cottages in the Court fell vacant, J.T.B. and his friends decided that the time was ripe for taking action different from the usual gospel mission, for it was (they thought) pretty hopeless trying to get at the souls of men through such a thick coating of filth: something more was needed.

'We rented the cottages and fumigated, debugged, distempered, and thoroughly cleaned them out. We brought in furniture, books for a library, games, etc., and so began Ashton's Court Mission. It had its Sunday service, educational classes for youth of both sexes, and work among the womenfolk. It was what is called today a community centre and youth club. Once the people of the Court understood that we weren't well-off folk doing a bit of slumming, they took to the idea and began to ask us to help them in their troubles. I remember being implored to visit a house where a youth of about fifteen was suffering from lung trouble; he later died. I shall never forget the sight. He was lying on a rough bed of sacks on the ground, in a filthy downstairs room, the windows were sealed, a large fire was burning in the grate, a sickening atmosphere enveloping everything.

'Despite our precautions in the preparation of the Mission Rooms, we occasionally spotted bugs crawling about and had to kill them. Trottie Horton and Lucy Allott were close companions in this work, and Lucy (who later became my wife) has

Cathedral City in the 'Nineties

told me that when returning home from the Court they would slip into a dark passage, take off their outer garments, and shake them vigorously to remove any unwelcome insects. Neither dared to inform their parents of the work they engaged in on one evening a week. Great was the horror of Lucy's step-mother when on one occasion she discovered a bug in Lucy's bedroom.

'Ashton's Court has been demolished now, its place taken by pleasant flats with garden plots about. In the 'nineties many choice young spirits responded to the need there. The work aroused our social consciousness. We were determined to put an end to such evils.'

Though still a Liberal, J.T.B. was increasingly conscious of the power of the words and example of such Socialists as William Morris, who declared that it was necessary to stir up the working class to demand a higher standard of life 'not merely for the sake of themselves, and the material comfort it will bring, but for the good of the whole world and the regeneration of the conscience of man'.

William Morris was doubly J.T.B.'s hero because he was the greatest craftsman of that age. He was a revolutionary in English design as well as in English politics. His speeches and writings were packed with sentiments that appealed to the lively imagination of James Thomas Baily.

'My cause,' said Morris, 'is the democracy of art, the ennobling of daily and common work which will one day put hope and pleasure in the place of fear and pain as the forces which move men to labour and keep the world going.'

A Utopian dream? Not to the sturdy young craftsman whose responding idealism sprang from the bench and the Bible, who felt the tide of life strong within him.

At twenty-one his apprenticeship was completed. He continued working at Lansdown's as a journeyman and he still attended evening classes at the Technical School. One evening he was bending over his desk, doing some advanced geometry, when his tutor, Mr Oldershaw, spoke to him. Sam Oldershaw had acquired a national reputation as a trainer of teachers in handicrafts. The idea that crafts should rightly be part of a general education was spreading through England.

'I've had a letter from St Albans in Hertfordshire,' said Mr Oldershaw. 'They need a teacher there, at their Technical Institute. You'd be doing building trades and manual training.'

Manual training was the then fashionable term for woodwork for boys, the new idea. A jumble of thoughts raced through the young man's head. This seemed a heaven-sent opportunity to bring together all the threads of his character and upbringing—the craftsmanship, the idealism, the excitement of tackling something new and big and *necessary*, as he fervently believed the crafts to be necessary for 'the ennobling of daily and common work'. But had he the capacity for so drastic a translation, from builder's journeyman to teacher? Oldershaw reassured him. He knew about J.T.B.'s work in Ashton's Court, the way he had managed the tough youths there, his zest, the loyalty he had won from young people.

'This is your chance, Jim,' he said. 'This is your vocation, or I'm a Dutchman.'

In due course a nervous young man was summoned before the Education Committee at St Albans. They required him to demonstrate mortice-jointing to a class of boys—then he sat before the committee to be interviewed.

'But the one question I most feared was not asked—my age. I was only twenty-one, and the post was one of some responsibility. I was appointed to the job, at £90 a year.'

The door had opened.

Twenty-six years later Mr Oldershaw turned up, when nearly seventy years of age, at the 1923 annual conference of the National Association of Manual Training Teachers at Cheltenham. By now this profession was properly organized, recognized, and qualified. 'Daddy' Oldershaw was greeted as one of its fathers; he went round shaking hands with his old protégés. One of them was the organizer of the 1923 conference, James Thomas Baily.

One of J.T.B.'s last acts before leaving Lincoln in 1897 was to purchase an engagement ring and slip it onto the finger of Lucy Allott.

'I paid for the ring out of a loan that an uncle made me to give me a start in my new position at St Albans. How rash is a young man in love.'

V

The Broadening Quest

St Albans was drowsing in the midday sun when J.T.B. first saw it. A row of idle carriages stood in tree-lined St Peter's Street, the horses drooping over their nose-bags as they waited for eternity or for something to turn up. The Abbey's long nave rose through a golden haze beyond the meadows where once the Romans built a city on the ageless road that runs from London to the heart of England and so to Holyhead. That road, and St Albans with it, was now enjoying its last nineteenth-century snooze before its twentieth-century awakening. Occasionally a farm wagon or a carrier's cart stirred its dust into a drifting cloud; very rarely the dusty whirlwind thrown up by a horseless carriage brought heads to windows as a staccato roar echoed through the dreaming streets of the town and startled the unready horse into sudden panic and precipitate flight.

Between the trees of the town one caught glimpses of the red-brick residences of prominent citizens, lawyers, estate agents, and doctors, with here and there some offices and a few shops. On one corner was the 'Gossip Shop', a tobacconist's, the daily rendezvous of worthies who exchanged their weighty views upon the city's affairs. Next to it was the barber's shop where you could be shaved for three-ha'pence.

Straw-hat making was the chief industry. To some extent it was still a cottage industry; a familiar sight was to see women carrying piles of finished hats to the warehouses, and returning home with bundles of straw plait. The fashion for men's straw 'boaters' and the rococo millinery of the late-Victorian woman kept this industry prosperous for the time being.

St Albans was popular as a dormitory town for London.

The Broadening Quest

Morning and night a black-coated and tall-silk-hatted army filled several trains to and from St Pancras. To become 'something in the city' was frequently the highest ambition parents had for their boys. To engage in any manual occupation was thought correspondingly low. It was not surprising, therefore, that soon after J.T.B. started teaching at the Manual Training Centre he received a letter from the mother of an eleven-year-old boy requesting that her son should be excused taking 'carpentry' because on leaving school he would not have to 'work' for his living.

Opposition to the new practical lessons at school came not only from the genteel. Zealous economists wrote to the St Albans newspaper declaring that, as ratepayers, they considered it a waste of money to extend the school curriculum beyond the three R's, which had been good enough in days gone by and should be good enough for future generations. The opposition that J.T.B. least expected came from men of his own class and type, from craftsmen who feared that the general teaching of crafts would overcrowd the labour market.

'One trade unionist wrote that my classes were going to take the bread out of the mouths of working men. A long correspondence ensued between us in the newspapers. It did something, I think, to establish in the public mind that in teaching boys to use their hands skilfully I was not necessarily training them for a manual vocation, any more than the teaching of history is intended to turn boys into professional historians. Ultimately the man who had started this scare wrote to say that he had not understood the true purpose, and he wished me well in my work.'

It will be gathered that the young teacher had an exceptionally clear conception, for that time, of the purpose of including the arts and crafts in a general education. Even today, sixty years later, it is all too rarely understood.

While keeping his eyes on the target, J.T.B. had to keep his nose to the grindstone, for he was well aware that his teaching qualifications were nil, apart from his natural abilities; all free evenings found him in his tiny bedroom studying for his Board of Education diplomas.

Craftsman and Quaker

'My lodgings cost 17s. a week. The food was plain but well cooked, though I did get somewhat of a surfeit of rice and prunes. The only light was from candles. In the winter I suffered much from cold, there being no fireplace or other means of heat, so I sat in my overcoat with a travelling rug round my knees, and when my fingers became numbed I held them round the candle flame and rubbed back the circulation.

'My first school workshop was two bare rooms with a minimum of benches and tools. Boys came to my centre for lessons from all the elementary schools in the city. I was far from satisfied with what we had to give them. I believed that a workshop should be attractive in appearance. I believed in visual aids. I believed in linking woodwork with other lessons ("integration" I suppose it would be called now). A boy making a mahogany book-rack could relate his woodwork lesson to his biology and geography, for on the walls of the workshop I arranged a collection of coloured lithographs of the trees of the world; there he could see what the mahogany tree looks like, on a map he was shown its geographical distribution, samples of its leaves were displayed under glass, and sections of its timber and seeds were exhibited, with an account of mahogany's various uses.'

This was indeed ahead of its time (how many schools are thus 'integrated' even today?). In four or five years the St Albans Centre became a show place, J.T.B. collected an armful of first-class teaching diplomas, and the work so expanded that he was given an assistant instructor. Visitors came from near and far to see what was happening, and the County Council invited Mr Baily to take additional classes for training handicraft teachers.

'One hot day I had an unexpected visitor, an elderly gentleman wearing a pith helmet and light linen clothes, and carrying a sunshade. He was a retired colonel of the Indian Army Medical Service, well-known in the city because of the unconventional attire he wore in the summer.

' "I've come", he declared, "to see what you're doing here. I like the look of it, sir. I think it's a good thing, this practical education. Wish I'd had such a chance myself."

The Broadening Quest

'A few days later he came again.

' "Been thinking about you, sir," he said. "And your work here. Like to give you something. Token of appreciation."

'I thanked him for his kind offer, and said I would think it over and would submit to him a list of things the school was needing most.

' "You misunderstand me," he replied. "I mean something for yourself."

'I said I would much prefer a gift for the school, and that this would make me happy too.

' "All right," he said. "Let me have your list."

'Greatly daring, I put as the first item on the list an expensive lathe. I can see him now, sitting in my study, looking at the illustration of the machine in the catalogue. He took from his pocket a little wash-leather bag and counting out a pile of golden sovereigns,

' "Buy the lathe," he said.

'Shortly after this he came again and placed in my hands two small parcels. "I do want you to have something personal," he insisted. The parcels contained a solid silver coffee pot and a small Indian jewel box made in teak, a lovely design decorated with finely executed carving.

' "Don't send any letters of thanks to my house," added the colonel. "And don't call to see me. I'm watched as a cat watches a mouse. I've had to bring those two gifts out by stealth. Dragon of a housekeeper. Jealous of my every action." '

In those last dreaming days no motor-bus services linked St Albans with the surrounding villages. Farmers' gigs arrived in the town laden with fruit and vegetables, eggs, butter, cheeses, poultry and rabbits. Lucy Baily sometimes bought half a side of bacon in the market.

Sunday would see J.T.B. walking through the Hertfordshire lanes. He never learned to ride a bicycle, despite the great bicycle boom. These were the weekends when droves of cyclists of both sexes sped between the whitened hedgerows to find adventure and romance on two wheels. The bicycle was the enemy of all chaperons; it played its part in removing the old puritanical inhibitions between the sexes. And it liberated townsfolk who had never known the smell of hay or the song of the thrush.

But J.T.B. preferred his two feet. All his life he enjoyed walking. His Sunday afternoon tramps in Hertfordshire had a twofold purpose, to enjoy the countryside and to preach in the village chapels under the care of the St Albans Congregational Church. Then he walked back to his dark-haired new wife Lucy in the new house they had had built, and for which he was himself making furniture in good English oak.

He had bought a frock coat and a tall silk hat. He had entered the middle-class.

'St Albans was a very class-conscious community. It was like a three-layer cake. At the top was the aristocratic layer, ornamented by such figures as the Earl of Verulam, Lord Grimthorpe, Lord Aldenham, Sir Blundell Maple, the Salisbury family at nearby Hatfield, and of course the bishop. They all had their carriages, their servants, and an unshaken belief that their natural place was on top of the cake. The Earl of Verulam I remember as resembling King Edward VII in appearance, as he drove in a coach-and-four on his way through St Albans from London to Gorhambury.

'The second layer in the cake, the middle-class, consisted of the city's men of commerce, doctors and solicitors and the like, with teachers just scraping in. This class also had its customs and etiquette, observed as strictly as those of the aristocrats. I remember on a Sunday morning how my wife and I would invariably meet Mr Gibbs, the printer, with his wife, en route to their chapel (Baptist) as we were on our way to ours. We always passed at the same point of intersection of our routes. He was a short patriarchal figure with long grey beard, dressed in frock coat and a flattish, almost clerical type of hat, and Mrs Gibbs, a grey little lady, was quite Victorian, with her arm in his. As we passed, Mr Gibbs and I would raise our toppers simultaneously and make a slight but gracious bow, bidding each other a good morning.

The Broadening Quest

'The third social stratum was the rapidly expanding working class. New industries were growing up, notably printing. Better education had produced throughout the country a wider reading public. Northcliffe's *Daily Mail* had introduced the "popular" Press. At St Albans our newspaper was one of the first in the provinces to set up on the new Linotype machines which had been introduced from America. Many printing businesses were established, on quite a large scale. These and other new industries caused great changes in the life of the city.'

The awakening town of St Albans provides an example in miniature of what happened widely throughout Britain in the early years of this century. Industrialism brought new workpeople to settle in the old town, and this upset the ancient order of the three-tier cake. Many of the newcomers were strong trade unionists with Socialistic leanings. Their arrival led to the foundation of the St Albans Co-operative Society, of Workers' Education Association branches, of adult schools; it led to a demand for houses. The old city began to grow a new wing, to the east. This in turn led to new enterprise in transport.

'A Mr Cable, who supplied cabs and funeral equipage to order, started a small horse-bus service to and from the new housing estate. He was also under contract to supply horses for the local fire brigade, and when a fire broke out Mr Cable sometimes had to take the pair from the bus on its route, leaving the passengers stranded.'

A Mr Bennett opened a cycle-making factory and founded a Polytechnic. In this building the townsfolk saw their first moving pictures: 'They were indistinct, blurred, and quivering, and occasionally the film snapped, but we thought them a wonderful novelty. They were silent films, of course.'

This marked the beginning of mechanised entertainment and the waning of home-made pleasures. Until the cinema came to St Albans most people found their recreation in the home and the garden, and in visiting friends for parties and conversation. Those who could afford went occasionally to London to see a play or variety show.

Craftsman and Quaker

'The theatre and music hall had been considered to be places of ill-repute by the people among whom I was brought up,' said J.T.B. 'I do not know that my parents ever went to any performance, and it was not until I was in my early twenties that I attended a play in a theatre. I then saw Forbes Robertson in *The Passing of the Third Floor Back*, and I was deeply moved by it.'

He also went to see Harry Lauder, the Scots comedian with the twisty walking stick, and from then on Lauder's song 'I love a lassie, a bonnie Hielan' lassie' was in the repertoire of ballads and comic ditties that J.T.B. took with him to parties. Though earnest in his application to the ideals he held dear, he had a native sense of humour to balance the puritanism of his upbringing. Life was real, life was earnest, but life was also genial.

There was a general air of geniality about in the Britain of the early years of this century, for the colourful reign of King Edward VII had begun. It was a hopeful time for all that generation who believed that the progress of mankind was inevitable as commerce and science expanded on all sides, and as the worst of the social evils were being tackled. A Liberal government had been returned in the 'landslide' election of 1906, and they seemed really intent on reform. For the young teacher making a swift success of his job, life seemed good.

Children were born to Lucy and James T. Baily (three boys); clockwork trains and Meccano sets and *The Children's Encyclopaedia* marked the passing birthdays, and the bass voice singing 'I love a lassie' or 'The Galloping Major' rang through the house from the little workshop in the attic where J.T.B. planed and sang, as his fathers had worked and rejoiced before him.

Of the threat from abroad, the increasing conflict of international jealousies, he and his generation were aware, of course; they knew of the arms race but were not acutely apprehensive. Their eyes were turned inward to Britain's smiling lot, and it *was* a smiling lot for many people who lived in the last rosy haze of insularity before Blériot's aeroplane buzzing across the Channel shattered our sense of security for ever.

The Broadening Quest

The long school summer holidays saw J.T.B. and his wife and children entraining for the seaside in those sunset days of nigger minstrels and bathing machines. Often he taught at summer schools for the training of teachers, held at such places as Yarmouth or Folkestone, and thus he combined duty with pleasure.

In his teaching he constantly stressed the need to link design with craftsmanship. A piece of woodwork or metalwork should be not only well made, but beautiful. Design was not his own strongest ability, for he had had no art training, but his perception of the right way to go about things was again ahead of his time. All through his life he dreamed of a school where the art teacher would work in complete collaboration with the craft teacher, but it was a dream that never quite came true.

He had a strong sense of historic continuity in the crafts. He had first seen it in the work of his grandfather and his father, and later it had been revealed to him in full glory at Lincoln Cathedral. Now, at St Albans, renewed inspiration was to be found in the abbey:

'I was particularly interested in the beautiful restoration of the fifteenth-century altar screen, known as the Wallingford Screen, with its exquisite tracery. This was done at the expense of Lord Aldenham and carried out by a wonderful craftsman of Exeter, Harry Hems, whom I got to know well. In his early life Harry had fulfilled the old tradition of being a journeyman craftsman; he had followed up his apprenticeship by going on the road to secure employment, travelling widely in other countries. He told me that while in Germany he was afraid his money might be stolen, and he hit upon a trick to use his mason's mallet as a "safe": taking out the shaft, he cut a part of the mallet's inside away, and into the vacant space he put his funds.'

Another noble peer of St Albans, Lord Grimthorpe, is said to have spent £130,000 on restorations at the abbey: 'He did so in the teeth of acute controversy, much of what he did as an amateur architect being severely criticised by professional architects and others, as being out of keeping with the character of the abbey.'

Craftsman and Quaker

Lord Grimthorpe was an eccentric, an amateur architect, a Q.C., and a clockmaker. He designed the Big Ben clock for the Houses of Parliament. During his restorations at St Albans a mason carved a portrait head of his lordship among the angels in one of the cathedral porches. The mason said that as his lordship was paying the piper he ought to be permanently preserved there in stone. J.T.B. once heard an American visitor remark: 'Well, it's the first time I've seen an angel wearing side-whiskers!'

More than eleven hundred years ago Benedictine monks founded the abbey in honour of St Alban, the first Christian martyr in England. In the tower of the present building you may see thin red Roman bricks taken from the ruined buildings of Verulamium, and not far away is the theatre where citizens were entertained in the years of the Caesars. Saxon, Norman and Gothic builders have left their mark on town and abbey.

In 1907 this history came to life. St Albans fell into the fashion of mounting a mammoth open-air pageant. Perhaps it was the prevalent conception of Britain's imperial greatness, passed on from Victorian to Edwardian times, that gave these pageants a vogue in many towns and cities before the First World War. The Boer War had cured the English of some of their jingoism, but they still had a strong sense of their historic destiny, and this was underlined by the pageants. Pageantry also appealed to everyone's love of dressing-up and play-acting. Citizens who were 'something in the city' swopped toppers and striped trousers for helmets and suits of armour, and rode through the town and streets on huge cart horses, caparisoned for battle, en route for the arena in the meadows where the ruins of Verulamium still stand.

When J.T.B. was asked to be assistant property master, which meant supervising the making of thousands of 'props', he fell into the work with gusto, capping it by marching on during the War of the Roses clad as an armourer of the Lancastrians:

'I wore an apron of cowhide and carried what appeared to be a heavy sledge-hammer; it was actually a light-weight shaft with an empty box of wood on its end. Showers of arrows passed

The Broadening Quest

overhead from the Yorkists stationed just beyond the end of the grandstand, and then the combatants closed in for hand-to-hand fighting, what time boys from the Grammar School who were hidden behind the Roman wall belaboured the iron railings there with pieces of iron tubing. So, with noises off, the Battle of St Albans was re-fought, not without casualties. We had a repair shop under the grandstand where a party of my pupils in relays were in attendance each day to repair broken properties.

'Many of the episodes were finely staged. Queen Boadicea, who was cheered nightly in her madly-galloping chariot, was played by a local farmer's daughter who had a reputation for daring horsemanship when riding after hounds, and she certainly lived up to her reputation.'

In days when the cinema was still a toy, pageants such as this were the nearest approach in spectacle, colour, sound and fury, to the movie marvels which have since taken their place. They were organized on a grand scale. Historians, musicians, and producers worked in teams on their presentation. A vacant straw-hat factory in St Albans was taken over as workshops and administrative offices. J.T.B. supervised the making of shields, swords, armour, pikes, halberds, maces, bows and arrows, the bier and coffin for Queen Eleanor's funeral, and even the music stands for the London Symphony Orchestra. Children knitted coats of 'chain mail' with string, which were then dipped in a rust-coloured dye and lightly faced on the outside with aluminium paint.

For J.T.B. it was fun making the 'props'. But his own heart was concerned deeply with other things than bygone wars and the remembered pomp of ancient kings. The Sunday top-hat and frock coat which symbolized his translation into the middle-class had not altered the man. Under the topper was a mind acutely and even agonisingly sensitive to the social strife within modern England; beneath the frock coat was a heart that ached at injustice. The smiling lot that had come his way, his share of Edwardian Britain's happiness, had not softened the sensibilities forged in a working-class Christian home. His attitude to social and political problems sprang directly from his religion, and that of course got him into trouble:

'There was a movement among bolder spirits in some of the Nonconformist churches at this time to align religion with social reform. This roused the protests of people who held that "you must not introduce religion into business", and certainly not into politics. This attitude seemed to me to be hypocrisy. My father and mother had taught me that life was religion, and religion life.'

Several things happened now to turn J.T.B. into a Socialist. One day a friend of his, a bricklayer, told him he had lost his job. His employer had fired him for enlisting fellow-workers into a trade union.

'Not only that, Jim,' said the unemployed bricklayer, 'they've blacklisted me.'

This meant that other employers in the town had been notified not to take him on. The injustice of it angered J.T.B.

He had been reading the novels of H. G. Wells. He was at once entranced and disturbed by the romantic story of young Kipps, the draper's apprentice who worked six days a week all the year round, with no fixed hours and no early-closing day, living-in at Shalford's Drapery Bazaar in conditions of prison-like gloom and restriction. He wondered how far this could be true.

Proof of its complete truth came right home, from Lucy Baily's brother. Percy Allott was a Kipps in real life. From the Allott home at Lincoln he had gone up to London, apprenticed to the stationery trade. He now told J.T.B. of the sweated labour and of the sordidness of living-in, as he had himself experienced it. This revelation lay heavily on J.T.B.'s mind; he dwelt upon it as another man might fret about the state of his roses or the fate of England in the Test Matches.

Percy Allott was one of the Angry Young Men of the Edwardian era. Determined to end the slavery he had himself endured, he became a full-time organizer for the Shop Assistants' Union, twice stood for Parliament, and spent his life and health at this work. But that is another story.

8

An example of litho-engraving done in Knockaloe: a New Year greeting card, 1918

Clock made at Knockaloe for Mr. W. J. Bassett-Lowke

The tools improvised by prisoner-of-war Wildmann, and two of the exquisite boxes he carved with them

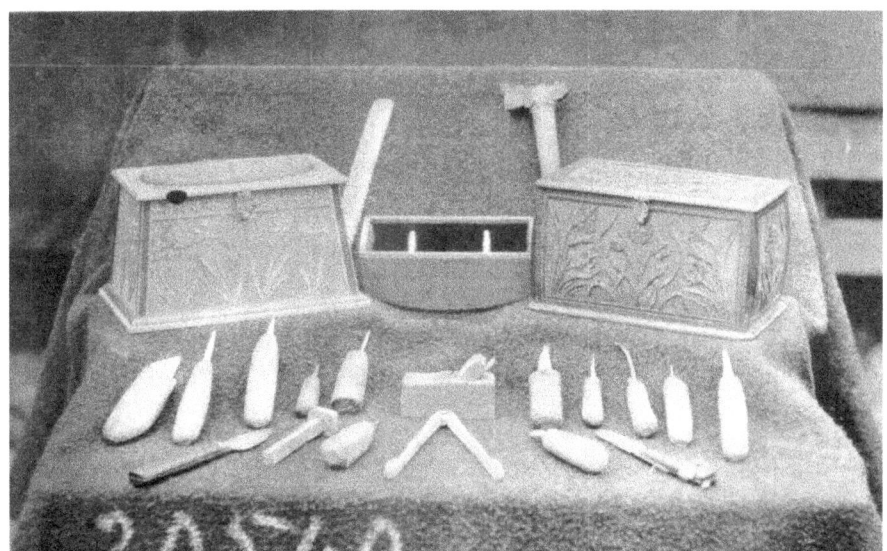

9
Food ticket issued at Frankfort-on-Main for 'Quakerhilfe' during J. T. B.'s visit to Germany in 1920

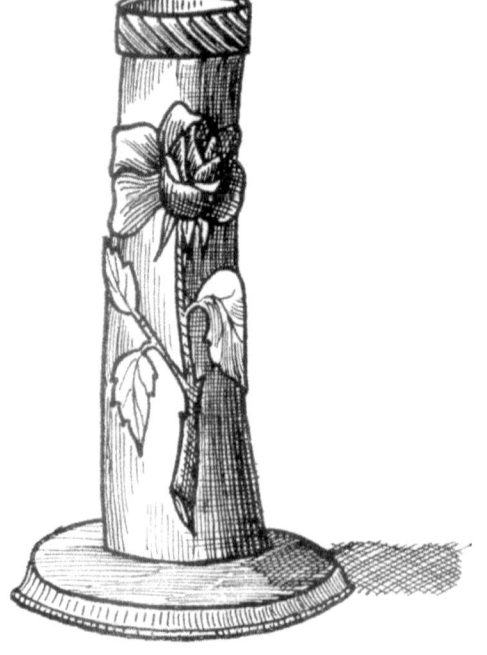

Vase carved from a marrow bone at Knockaloe internment camp, Isle of Man

The Broadening Quest

For J.T.B. the revelation coincided with the Sweated Industries Exhibition held at the Queen's Hall in London. It was organized in 1906 by *The Daily News*, the cost being borne by that devoted champion of social reform, the Quaker industrialist, George Cadbury. A series of tableaux showed workers in various trades: girls making shirts at less than a penny an hour; bunching violets at 7d. a gross; hook-and-eye carding at 1s. 4d. for 384 hooks and 384 eyes. A man was shown making chains: a heavy day's work of eleven hours earned him 6s. to 8s. a week. The pay for making match boxes was 2$\frac{1}{2}d$. a gross.

Today these figures may seem unbelievable. They were true half a century ago. The consequences in terms of squalor, malnutrition, disease and prostitution may easily be imagined.

'I went up to London and spent most of a day at the exhibition,' said J.T.B. 'I was horrified. I had seen sordid industrialism in Sheffield, but I had not realized until now just how sordid it could be.'

It revolted his sense of Christian values. It outraged his deepest ideals as a craftsman. Industrial slavery was the negation of craftsmanship.

Many working-class boys passed through J.T.B.'s school workshops. Sometimes he despaired how little he could do for them. Was it any use hoping that by teaching them to make good and beautiful things with their hands they might come within sight of the William Morris Utopia, 'the ennobling of daily and common work which will one day put hope and pleasure in the place of fear and pain'? The industrial Moloch had created a darkness that seemed impervious to such ideals.

Sometimes hope faded. But always it revived.

The approach to Utopia must be through the schools, in which the arts and crafts should be taught as vigorously and well as the sciences and languages, but that was not enough. The attack must be on many fronts, including the political. Here the outlook was getting brighter. Spirits rose with a series of victories all along the social security front. Winston Churchill, Home Secretary in the new Liberal Government, tackled the sweated industries,

Craftsman and Quaker

with his Trade Boards Act. William Beveridge pioneered unemployment and health insurance. Old-age pensions were introduced by Lloyd George in 1909. Powers were taken for the clearance of slums. Things moved fast in the exciting years between 1906 and 1914.

For the first time a government interfered in the conditions and hours of work in coal mines. Even the poor forgotten Kippses were remembered when shop assistants were guaranteed (in 1912) a half-holiday every week.

Behind the leaders of reform marched many stalwart souls who gave much time and thought to agitating, writing, and speaking for the new Jerusalem they aspired to build in England's partially green and occasionally pleasant land, and J.T.B. was one of these.

Yet he was dissatisfied: 'I grew impatient with the Liberal Party. It had a reactionary wing which distrusted Lloyd George and Winston Churchill and the other vigorous reformers. At the same time this was a period when the Labour Party was in full fight. They were now twenty-nine strong in the House of Commons. I became convinced that they understood the lot of the common people better, and were striving for reforms harder than the Liberals, who I thought were at times reluctant as a party to champion measures that would cost their class something. Pacifism was another factor in swaying me towards the Socialists. I felt that they were out-and-out for peace, whereas the Liberals were compromised by their imperialist wing. The strong spirit of Christian idealism in such Labour leaders as Keir Hardie and George Lansbury attracted me.'

So now pacifism for the first time comes seriously into his mind, as he enters his thirties and the years tick on towards 1914. The broadening of his philosophy is taking a fateful and perhaps a dangerous turn. Look back for a moment over the way this man has come. He began simply enough, inheriting a delight in craftsmanship for its own sake, for the shaping of wood with chisel, the sheer joy of creating. Then, from the vantage point of a working-class home in an industrial city, he saw the malignant effect of industrialism on craftsmanship, and he became a teacher

The Broadening Quest

not merely to give to others his skills but because he now shared the Utopian dream of William Morris, that the people must recapture their inheritance, their creative genius; those who could not use it in the factories and offices of a robot world might be taught the enthusiasm and ability to do so in their leisure. But the bog of industrialism was deeper than the young man had bargained for. The sin of poverty, as Bernard Shaw declared, was the worst of all sins because it bred every other social evil. What hope for a right use of leisure in such conditions? The attack on poverty must be political and nation-wide. Our questing young man became a Socialist. His religious upbringing argued that the social system was un-Christian; it must be changed for religious as well as for political reasons, by religious methods as well as political. Politics must enter into religion. Religion must enter into politics. Politics (applied Christianity) must reach towards the Utopian ideal, must totally remove the social evils of our country, so that the skills and ideals we teach the nation's children shall no longer be wasted and blunted by the dreariness and materialism of the grown-up world with its climate of fear and victimisation.

So far had the quest broadened.

But now J.T.B. heard Keir Hardie's warning: 'Militarism and all that pertains to it is inimical to the cause of progress, the well-being of the people, and the future of the race.'

Britain had been making alliances, in the Edwardian period, with France and Russia. Germany was lined up with Austria-Hungary. As bigger and better battleships were launched on either side, a revived jingoism was stimulated in these sabre-rattling years. Keir Hardie denounced the alliances, arguing that they would intensify the international climate of fear and make war more, not less, likely. If the ordinary average man was not as worried as Keir Hardie it was because there was no precedent of world war to warn him of the consequences. In the burning summer of 1911, when King George V was crowned and the people gloried in the seemingly ever-increasing power and prosperity of Britain, few foresaw the mass carnage to come four or

Craftsman and Quaker

five years later. It was not so much apprehension of economic and physical disaster, therefore, that made J.T.B. a pacifist; it was a realization that war must be opposed for the same reasons as the social evils within the nation: because militarism was created by, and in turn created, an atmosphere of fear, brute force, and greed; and because these were incompatible with the Sermon on the Mount.

Peace, in short, was indivisible. Peace and love within the family circle; peace and fair-dealing within the nation; peace and goodwill between all nations: these were widening aspects of the same thing, the Kingdom of God. To bring it on earth must surely *mean* 'on earth', not in one's own country alone, not just for one class of society.

This broadening outlook was bound to lead to trouble.

The Boer War had already sharpened J.T.B.'s youthful misgivings about warfare. He was not surprised that the vast majority of British people had no qualms of conscience as the fighting dragged on into worsening ferocities and finally to the demand for 'unconditional surrender', but to see almost all the leaders of almost every church on that side perplexed him. He found his sympathies going out to the few people who opposed the campaign in South Africa either for political reasons, as Lloyd George did, or on account of religious convictions, as did one or two of his friends who were Quakers. They belonged to a church—the Society of Friends—that was traditionally pacifist; they told him that not all Quakers were against *this* war, but that the Society as a whole had declared its firm opposition in a public statement: 'We fail to see how any war can be waged in the Spirit of Jesus Christ.'

This was the sort of yardstick that J.T.B. found himself applying to life. But in the turbulent years that followed the Boer War—the Edwardian years of industrial unrest, the years when the Liberal Government was striving to bring about social justice—J.T.B. ran into bewilderment as he tried to square moralities with realities. When industrial strikers brought the nation almost to a standstill he asked whether this use of force could be justi-

The Broadening Quest

fied. And what about the suffragettes?—but for the militant methods they were using would they be likely to gain the plain justice of votes for women? Could expediency ever be permitted to interfere with principle? Did the end ever justify the means? Surely the Christian yardstick must always be applied? To such questions J.T.B. expected religious leaders to give a clear answer. As so often happens, the quest for truth led into the wilderness.

For two years J.T.B. was almost without faith: 'I felt that men of religion had failed me.'

No longer did he go down every Sunday morning to church, or tramp the Hertfordshire lanes to the outlying chapels. A new minister had come to the St. Albans church where he was a deacon, and the two men's ideas clashed in a conflict we will not attempt to resurrect. All J.T.B. would say of it later was this: 'I was rather hasty tempered. I had a strong group of young members ready to support me but, fearing to split the church, I declined to carry the dispute further, and resigned office and any further participation in the church's affairs. Faced with what I felt to be intolerance and clerical rigidity, I reacted by questioning the whole of religious faith.'

Some of the institutional and ceremonial aspects of religious practice seemed, on analysis, to be unrelated to the simple teaching of the carpenter of Nazareth: 'Prayers, I thought, sometimes included much that was meaningless and even incompatible with the idea of a Father of everlasting and all-abounding love. The same applied to hymns:

> Take my silver and my gold,
> Not a mite would I withhold.
> Take my intellect and use
> Every power as Thou shalt choose . . .

'Singing this, I asked myself: "Do I and others really mean all that the words imply? Aren't we making mental reservations, or excusing the words as symbolic and not to be taken literally?"'

Craftsman and Quaker

Doubt has a habit of spreading. 'I began to question the suitability of a rigid order of service—hymns, prayers, sermons—for a whole congregation, irrespective of their individual states of mind and spiritual development. It might suit some people, but it seemed not to suit me. There was one good pastor I knew whose sermons were homely and occasionally helpful, but so often dull and uninspired. "How," I thought, "can any man feel absolutely sure of bearing a Divine message twice each Sunday and once on a weekday evening, year in and year out?" '

Dull sermons were bad enough; sermons that were unrelated to the chronic social issues at home and abroad were worse. This did not seem to J.T.B. to be what Christianity was for.

He began to take a more detached view of religious observance. He saw how easy it was merely to go through the motions, for he had so often done it himself. On Sundays now he was frequently to be found at the St Albans Adult School, where men of all classes and types met together—a bricklayer sat next to a Royal Academician, boot-manufacturer and shop assistant, employer and employed, Tories, Liberals, Socialists, churchmen and agnostics, they took part in discussions on religious and political and other topics, and if the argument raged too stormily it was the Quaker president, Alfred Lynn, who poured oil on the waters. Nation-wide, the adult school movement was vigorous in these years, and many Quakers were prominently associated with it. J.T.B. found their company congenial. The Quaker record in social service, ranging around such peaks of unselfish achievement as Elizabeth Fry's work to improve prisons and John Woolman's opposition to slavery, appealed to the young man who had once aspired to be a missionary. The Quaker attitude to war seemed refreshingly consistent to a young man impatient with the inconsistencies around him.

'Back in my 'teens I had heard a young Quakeress, Mary Spencer, speak at Lincoln on War and Peace, and I had never forgotten her challenge to human vacillations on this issue. She had said quite firmly and quite simply that a Christian could have no part whatever in war, because every human being had within

The Broadening Quest

him something of God. By virtue of this "Inner Light", shed abroad in every human soul, all men, of whatever race or nation, were brothers. I thought it must be hard to carry this belief into consistent practice, but it struck some deep chord in my own make-up.'

One Sunday during what he afterwards called his spell in the wilderness, J.T.B. followed Alfred Lynn into the Quaker meeting. He felt shy and conspicuous as he slipped into one of the seats where people were assembled in silence, but no one stared. There was no rolling organ music. The room was plain to the point of austerity. There was no pre-set order of service. There was no parson. Occasionally the silence was broken as a man or woman rose to speak or to pray. At first the long silences between were disconcerting; a fly buzzed at the window, one felt a self-conscious urge to cough and fidget. Then something said by the last speaker would seem to permeate the ensuing silence with overtones of meaning; then perhaps the fly buzzed again and one's attention was distracted. But when J.T.B. went away from the meeting, a little puzzled, he felt happier in spirit than he had been for a long while.

He went back into the quiet Meeting House again and again, as the Sundays came round.

At first he missed the singing, for despite his frequent dislike of the words of hymns he had always enjoyed singing and the glorious sense of spiritual release it can give. But what was lost here was more than gained in the candour and depth of the informal spoken ministry . . . or at least it was gained sometimes. Other times he was overwhelmed by misgivings.

In a sense, he missed the parson: 'I gathered that the Quakers believed that the Voice of God can speak through anyone: any individual in the meeting for worship was potentially a minister. But if all and sundry were free to speak did this not offer a tiresome opportunity to cranks and duffers? How could one be sure it *was* the Voice of God? I found by experience that one couldn't. There were occasions when the cranks ground their axes and the duffers were as uninspired as any treadmill parson I'd ever heard.

Craftsman and Quaker

With a little more tolerance and experience I was to learn that the dross can contain gold if you look for it, but at the start there was this problem. The Quakers have no ordained ministry. The spiritual and intellectual worth of what is said in a Quaker meeting must hang perilously, I argued, on the personal qualities of the speaker, his knowledge of life, his spiritual insight, his understanding of the Bible. It was a matter of chance whether such people might be found in any meeting. Admittedly, the sermons I had heard in the past from many ordained ministers of several denominations had shown that it was not a matter of certainty that they were inspired, but if, in a Quaker meeting, *every* individual was potentially a minister, then it followed that each member must try to bring himself by study and by his way of life to the standard one would expect of a good minister. This filled me with doubts.'

Was Quakerism perhaps a bit too much of a good thing?

To apply the gospel of love to all of life seemed a gospel of perfection. He was not perfect, and would be ill-fitted to join a society of perfectionists.

For some time the pools of silence were difficult to negotiate; he felt like a learner hanging back at the edge of a swimming pool, repelled by the water and yet attracted, envying the swimmers and yet wondering what they could enjoy in it. Then in some mysterious way it was no longer a silence but a voice speaking inwardly.

'In the silence I prayed for guidance. Then one Sunday morning Elizabeth Lynn, mother of Alfred Lynn, as she passed to her place in meeting, put her hand on my shoulder where I sat and whispered in my ear, "Quench not the Spirit!" She was a woman of singular intuition and had sensed my spiritual condition. I felt it was God's guidance.

'And so I became a Quaker. After all the trouble at the Congregational Church there came a happy ending. Hearing of my being received into membership of the Society of Friends, they wrote a warm letter of recommendation. This completely removed any bitterness that still remained.

The Broadening Quest

'And soon I felt very much at home among the Quakers. The main thing about Quakerism which attracted me, and has held me, can be expressed quite simply. It is that the spirit of God is in every man, woman, and child, and may be expressed through all of life.'

VI

From Brooklyn to Borstal

Eight days out from England, the White Star liner *Teutonic* crept up Long Island Sound towards the famous skyline of New York. The tallest skyscraper, the Flatiron Building as people called it rather unkindly, was only twenty-one storeys high, but to the three English school teachers who stood on the liner's deck the perpendicular city advancing through the morning mist was an out-of-this-world vision—'Futuristic' they might have called it three or four years later, but in 1906 that word had not been invented. In many ways a visit to America was like stepping into the future for the Edwardian Englishman: 'The first time I walked down Broadway it seemed like walking in a deep canyon, and the roar and rush of the traffic, both from the street and the elevated railway, was a new sensation after the mild clatter of a more leisurely London,' wrote J.T.B.

'I was impressed by the smart and well-fitted shops, but indoors I felt stifled by the heat. Central heating was already commonly used in American cities. The Americans were in some ways ahead of British practice in architecture, in household equipment, and in their superb transport facilities. The same applied in their schools.'

The schools were an eye-opener. The three travellers, Baily, Riley, and Johnstone, had come to investigate craft teaching, as members of the Mosely Commission. They brought back a report which alleged that by comparison our British schools were primitive in equipment and timid in their approach to this side of education. To be sure, the American schools the visitors inspected were show-places, as always happens with deputations to all

From Brooklyn to Borstal

countries, but it is doubtful whether the best American standard of fifty years ago has even yet been reached in Britain.

It would be interesting to know how far the superlative build-up of technological power in the USA during these years has been based on foundations well-laid in schools that approached the arts and crafts with as much enthusiasm and efficiency as the book-learning subjects.

The journey to America came as a powerful stimulus to J.T.B.'s ideas, focussing them on the future, so that he returned to England a 'futurist' in craft-teaching. His sponsor, Mr Alfred Mosely, was a City of London merchant who believed we had a lot to learn from American methods. He proposed to various educational bodies in Great Britain that they should send groups of investigators across the Atlantic. He bore most of the expense himself, and even beguiled the shipping company to provide second-class return passages for £5.

As soon as they landed, J.T.B. and his two colleagues were hustled off to a suite at Columbia University where they lived free. The first school they visited was the Manual Training High School, Brooklyn.

'The school has sixty microscopes coasting £6 apiece,' says an envious diary note. Even the timetable worked automatically, being connected to a clock (known as a Cylinder Programme Clock) which automatically rang a bell in each room when the class had to change for another lesson. But J.T.B. added:

'Equipment is not sufficient in itself. It is the teaching method that matters. In the art and craft rooms of this vast school the pupils are encouraged to think things out for themselves. The great thing is to evoke the interest of the pupil. The teachers are given freedom to devise their own schemes of tuition so long as they keep the end in view. As the Head, Dr Larkins, puts it: "If I send a messenger to the City Hall I guess I don't care how he gets there, whether by the bridge or the ferry, so long as he gets there in the time given, and with the right message." '

From Brooklyn to Boston, and on across the States and Canada, the Mosely Commission visited school after school, and the diary was rapidly filled with first impressions of methods which have since become fairly common on both sides of the Atlantic.

On discipline: 'Ideas here in America are very different from those of England. What we would regard as rude impertinence is only "sympathetic frankness". At Toronto University I attended evening classes for teachers at which the students were discouraged from the "lecture and sit-stiff business", as it is called.'

On 'integration': 'At Philadelphia we inspected the Manual Training High School where Mr Sayre is developing some of the most advanced methods in America. Drawing and design lessons are linked with woodwork, clay modelling, carving, and work in stone and metals. In the large classes I did not see two students working alike. Individualism is encouraged.'

This was J.T.B.'s own pet principle carried farther than he could possibly approach it in Britain, for lack of facilities and funds. How he envied these Americans!

'At Springfield, Massachusetts, we saw some boys making a large canoe: an excellent piece of craft-teaching, for a canoe is a thing that will attract the enthusiasm of boys, its construction involves many aspects of craftsmanship, and the finished article is a thing of beauty and of exciting utility.

'A model canal lock, complete with sluices, barges, etc. had been worked out in another school by children who were studying industrial problems.

'In another the boys had designed and made three printing presses, the early screw-press, a later toggle-jointed press, and another with a cam motion. This practical work was co-ordinated with their art lessons; they designed a cover for a book, made a block of their own design, and printed the cover off on their home-made press.

'We saw Sixth Grade boys making looms which were then handed over to Second Grade children (four years younger) who did weaving on them.'

At Albany: 'There is here an institution known as The Parents' and Teachers' Association. They meet together for social intercourse and discuss matters concerning their children's education.

From Brooklyn to Borstal

Some parents are appointed by the Association as official school visitors.'

Everywhere they went the Englishmen breathed the stimulating ozone of American life. And their trip was not all work: 'At Niagara Falls there was thick snow on the ground, and many degrees of frost. Heavily clothed, with thick gloves and helmet-like caps with ear-flaps, we piled into a horse-drawn sleigh to see the sights.

'Dismounting and walking to the edge of the gorge, we were greeted by a photographer: "Take home a photo of the falls, gentlemen. A wonderful souvenir! Let your friends see you standing before the greatest phenomenon of nature."

'Riley and I were in the mood to try this. We were surprised, however, when the photographer brought out an enlarged photographic print of the falls and placed it behind the spot where he had seated us. He then snapped us against this fake background. The photographs came out well, and are perhaps more convincing as "works of art" than they would have been had he tried to focus on us and Niagara at the same time.'

Before he left America, J.T.B. was offered a teaching position in one of their splendidly equipped schools. It was a strong temptation, but something stronger impelled him to return. Maybe it was the old missionary spirit. The report that he and his colleagues put in to Mr Mosely and to the Board of Education made drastic suggestions:

(1) That British regulations should be more elastic, should give teachers greater freedom to adapt schoolwork to the needs and capabilities of the child, and to the conditions of life in the district where the child lives;

(2) That craft work should be taken by every child uninterruptedly throughout its school career, and should be intimately correlated with other subjects;

(3) That a more complete and efficient training should be given to every craft teacher.

The first and third of these proposals have since been met; not so the second.

Craftsman and Quaker

In later years, when J.T.B. taught in English grammar schools, he was bitterly disappointed by the tendency to withdraw children from the workshops as they came towards the age, fifteen and upwards, when they had to sit their external examinations. Even when the university examiners permitted crafts to be taken this facility was not widely used, many grammar schools preferring to drive their boys and girls almost exclusively through the classics and the sciences to gain their leaving certificates, thus depriving them of continued art and craft training in the years when their creative faculties are reaching towards maturity, and when expression of these natural gifts could balance an excessively bookish life.

'Craft work should be taken by *every* child . . .' The democratic nature of American education was a thing that J.T.B. envied. The British habit of dividing schools into social or intellectual sections usually means that good art and craft teaching is denied to some boys and girls; to the end of his life J.T.B. insisted from his wide experience that it was nonsense to assume that a grammar school boy or a public school boy needed it less—or more—than a 'Secondary Modern type'.

Soon after his return from America the opportunity came to test his methods and his beliefs at the opposite ends of the English educational scale: in a public school and at Borstal.

'A red-letter day for me came in 1908. The headmaster of St Albans School invited me to introduce woodwork into the curriculum of his school, third oldest public school in the country, originating from A.D. 948. The English secondary and public schools were (with a few exceptions) slow to recognize the value of handicrafts, so this approach from the most venerable of them sounded to me like a victory. The headmaster, Mr Montague Jones, was a member of the Higher Education Sub-Committee for St Albans, by whom I was employed, and he had thus become familiar with my work at the Technical School, where I was now headmaster. For a workshop he offered me a beautiful room above the archway of the old Abbey Gate. We equipped it with benches and tools. In this mediaeval setting and with a fine

From Brooklyn to Borstal

King Charles fireplace as a feature of the room, I opened a new chapter in St Albans School's long history. It continued until I left St Albans in 1911. The headmaster was progressive, refusing to be fettered by old traditions when they retarded liberalising developments, and I was glad he used me to fulfil his ideas.'

Teaching in a prison was the opposite extreme of experience. This is how J.T.B. came to teach at Borstal. In 1911 he was asked by the Kent Education Committee to become handicrafts supervisor for the Medway towns of Rochester, Chatham, and Gillingham; he and his family moved house from St Albans to the village of Borstal which stands on a hill above the River Medway, outside Rochester. The country rises steeply from the wide mud flats (saltings) familiar to readers of Charles Dickens' *Great Expectations*, and crowning the hill is a grim old prison which was indeed known to Dickens, but where work has been done in modern times which would have astonished and delighted that great writer and social reformer. Boys between sixteen and twenty-three years of age who are sentenced to imprisonment are sent to this and other Borstal Institutions for periods of hard training and education with the object of reforming them and returning them into the world with the hope that they will become worthy citizens. The experiment began at Borstal in 1902 when it was recognized that juvenile offenders too old for reformatory school need special treatment if they are not to become habitual criminals.

Not long after J.T.B. went to live in Borstal village he climbed the hill to the prison and was admitted through the great iron-studded gate. For three evenings a week thereafter he tried to teach geometry and building construction to as tough a crowd of delinquents as ever a teacher faced. It was not easy; J.T.B. needed to call upon every particle of his patience, and to hold hard by his newly confirmed Quaker faith in 'that of God in every man'—the pious phrase came up for rough testing at times in Borstal, but J.T.B. never despaired. He had a strong sense of discipline which he could apply quite strictly and yet without prejudice to his deepest belief in the power of love. His 'boys' responded when they realized how much he was interested in their welfare.

'I knew that they came to evening classes tired after long and strenuous hours of work, so I tried to make my lessons very practical, to arouse and retain their interest. I found that many of them were intelligent chaps, and most of them did well in my classes.

'One evening I was approached by the Prison Chaplain who said that Robert Wilfred Dale, a Rochester City Councillor and a Quaker, had told him of my interest in Adult Schools.

' "I've been wondering whether we could start an Adult School for the Blue Bottles," said the Chaplain. (Blue Bottles was a nickname for the Blue Grade prisoners who wore a distinctive blue uniform of rough serge.) "The Governor agrees that it could be held at six o'clock each Sunday evening, provided that we can find a man suitable for a leader. Would you be willing to take the job on?" '

So began the first Adult School in a prison.

'We endeavoured, and I think successfully, to impress upon the boys the idea that it was their Adult School, so its success or failure depended upon their whole-hearted participation. My friend Headley Horsnaill and I kept as much as possible in the background, advising and drawing out promising talent. I, perforce, always presided but we soon had boys on their feet introducing the lesson of the day, and this would be followed by a lively discussion. When we began the experiment there was a prison regulation in force that a warder must be present, but I suggested to the Governor that his attendance should be dispensed with. He was withdrawn, and the trust shown thereby was never abused.'

Later, when J.T.B. left the district, the leadership of the Borstal Adult School was taken over by others; in 1934, to his delight, he received a programme which showed that that particular school for sinners was still going strong, with addresses on subjects as varied as 'Louis Pasteur', 'Bees and Bee Keeping',

10

Furniture made by Germans at Knockaloe for use in the French houses

Quaker relief workers building houses in France, 1918

11 Repatriation, 1919—as depicted in the Rhuleben camp magazine, by a British internee, and by a German artist at Knockaloe, Isle of Man

From Brooklyn to Borstal

'Oliver Cromwell', 'First Aid in Wartime', and 'Some Christmas Customs'—not to mention 'Never too late to Mend'!

In the evenings of 1912 and 1913 when the Borstal gate clanged behind him and he walked wearily down the hill to his home, J.T.B. little realized how soon his experience of handling men in prison was to come in useful in an utterly different context. European war was now only a matter of months away. There were thousands of men in Britain living peacefully enough—serving behind counters, playing in orchestras, tinkers, and tailors, rich men, and poor men—who were soon to be imprisoned as securely as the Borstal boys, but not because they had committed any crime, unless their crime was to have been born 'enemy aliens'.

The teacher walking home, dwelling on the trials and errors of his evening's work behind bars, could not in his wildest dream foresee this future. But nor could any of the millions soon to be caught up in the iron hand.

There was still a dream-like charm about the country around Rochester, the Garden of England, as that part of Kent was then so rightly called, its orchards splashed with pink and white in spring, its oast-houses peeping through the hop-fields, its whitened roads leading down to the lonely sands by the sea. There was a quietness along the beaches, and over the Downs the skylark sang almost unchallenged. Very occasionally—so infrequently that it was a nine-days wonder—a flying machine would drone across the sky; now and then a plume of dust would move between the hedges of a country road as a horseless-carriage banged along its way, flaunting its white banner of revolution behind it; but then the quietness of the ages would settle down again as the sun set across the lonely marshes and the labourer took home his sleepy horse.

The old city of Rochester still had a Dickensian atmosphere. Through its narrow streets one could well imagine the stage-coach bringing Mr Pickwick to the Bull Hotel. The cathedral and the Norman keep of the castle were reminders of yet older associations, and the River Medway's noble sweep round the castle ruins always gave a touch of romance to the scene, with the brown sails of a barge as decoration. Nearby, at Gad's Hill, Charles Dickens had lived and died in an old-fashioned, red-brick house.

There was another old-fashioned house, just across the river, at Strood. It is fixed in the memory with all the placid atmosphere of those pre-war days, like a photograph in an album—an upper-middle-class-Victorian villa with high sunny rooms and venetian blinds, its porticos giving on to a trim lawn where croquet was played and a shaggy sheep-dog lay in the shade of a cedar tree. At Yoke House lived the Horsnaills, a Quaker family with whom the Bailys made friends; and here is a last picture of the England that was soon to pass away, as J.T.B. remembered it in the years to come: 'The head of the family, Alfred Horsnaill, was a fine bearded figure of a man, a prosperous corn-merchant. His beautiful and charming wife, May, was one of the most lovable characters it has been my privilege to meet. Sundays at Yoke House were times for entertaining friends and visitors, and often a party of us would gather there for supper followed by music and singing. Headley would take a tenor part, his father and I would take bass parts. June, a daughter in her teens who was studying at the Royal Academy of Music, was at the piano. Another daughter, Ruth, played the 'cello, and the mother sang sweetly. It may appear that we were unsophisticated; yet what enjoyable times these were. We sang hymns from the Adult School Hymn Book and songs from the Scottish Students' Song Book, songs such as "Oh, hush thee my Baby" and "Excelsior" and "Drink to me only with thine eyes". Some of us would bring along our own pieces of music as solos. I would sing "Off to Philadelphia" or "Passing By".'

This picture of the pre-radio domestic days has a peculiar nostalgia, but it lacks a deeper quality that belonged to the Horsnaill home. Perhaps J.T.B. realized this when he added a footnote to his diary-paragraph on Yoke House:

'The Quakers have no written creed or dogma, but there are certain Advices which are read periodically in meetings for worship: they are suggestions for the guidance of one's conduct rather than inflexible rules laid down by a high authority. They derive from three centuries of common-sense experience of life, the Advices having been drawn up and issued occasionally from the earliest days of Quakerism, and revised from time to time. I am always reminded of the Horsnaill household by one of the Advices:

' "In your style of living, in your dress and in the furniture of your houses, choose what is simple and beautiful. Encourage the reading of good books, so that the taste thus formed may instinctively reject the base and trivial. Be mindful for yourselves and your children of the beauty and power of friendship. . . . Endeavour to make your home an abiding place of joy and peace, where the presence of God is known." '

J.T.B. found great happiness in his contact with the Quakers; it was an added and overflowing joy, as a teacher, to find that since its earliest days the Society of Friends had regarded education as part of the ministry of God, and, as a crafts teacher, to discover that the famous Quaker pioneer and statesman, William Penn, had written something about the teaching of craftsmanship two hundred years earlier which J.T.B. might himself have written (apart from the archaic language) in 1914. Of children Penn wrote, in *Some Fruits of Solitude*: 'We press their memory too soon, and puzzle, strain and load them with words and rules, to know grammer and rhetorick, and a strange tongue or two, that it is ten to one may never be useful to them, leaving their natural genius to mechanical and physical or natural knowledge uncultivated and neglected which would be of exceeding use and pleasure to them through the whole course of their life. . . . Children had rather be making of tools, and instruments of play, shaping, drawing, framing, building &c; than getting some rules of propriety of speech by heart; and those also would follow with more judgment, and less trouble and time.'

Oh, for a school where the hands should, as Rousseau said, 'work to the advantage of the intellect'!—where all our craftsman-missionary's experience, all he had seen in America, might be put to the trial. In his supervisory position to the Medway towns' schools J.T.B. tried to influence craft teachers, and he was never slow to spread his ideas by articles in technical journals and through textbooks for teachers. In 1913 he wrote in the preface of one of these that it was 'an attempt to show how light woodwork may be taught in the classroom, and how the practical work may be correlated with other subjects, especially with arithmetic, drawing, and composition".[1] Correlation was an advanced idea in the England of 1913, and J.T.B. found that State schools were too restricted by routine and regulation to permit drastic experimentation. The chance of having a hand in such a pioneering trial came through his new association with the Quakers.

The Society of Friends owns a group of boarding schools independent of the State. One of these had embarked in 1906 on a new and daring policy. Sibford School, in lovely Oxfordshire country on the edge of the Cotswolds, had a new headmaster, James T. Harrod, who introduced practical studies to an extent that was not then 'recognized' by the State. In the following year Sibford's experiment was applauded by Professor (later Sir) Michael Sadler, of Oxford University, who said in a speech at Sibford that some time in the future 'it is probable that such a course of training as you provide here will be recognized by the State as one kind of secondary education'. This has happened. The unique kind of secondary education offered at Sibford in 1906 was very similar to that adopted in 1944 by the State for its Secondary Modern Schools. Handwork, domestic science, nature study, and gardening had prominent places in the Sibford co-educational curriculum.

'A boy or girl,' said Mr Harrod, 'is better trained to think by associating action with thought than by the exclusively bookish forms of instruction.' He worked out a policy whereby such subjects as English, history, geography, and mathematics should be correlated as far as possible with manual training.

[1] *Light Woodwork* by J. T. Baily and W. G. Alderton (Arnold), 1913. See also *Woodwork* by J. T. Baily and S. Pollitt (John Murray), 1922.

From Brooklyn to Borstal

'Successful experimentation such as this,' said J.T.B., 'is a justification for the existence of private schools. I served on the Management Committee of Sibford School for some years and was glad to have an advisory part in the excellent work done there in those brave pioneering days.'

A disadvantage of independent schools in comparison with State schools is that the former may not possess the financial resources to carry a policy through to its utmost. Sibford never achieved the range of work, the equipment and staffing, that J.T.B. had seen in American pioneer schools. He dreamed of working some day in a school where all that was best might be found together—the financial resources of the State—the independence of vision of Sibford—and the practical example of the American schools. . . . What wonders might be achieved!

It was a noble vision. But now it was August 1914.

VII

The Red-and-Black Star

'I was spending my summer holiday of 1914 at Yarmouth, teaching woodwork at a Summer School for teachers. On August 5th we read the headlines of war between Great Britain and Germany, following the invasion of Belgium by the Kaiser's army. Next day I saw a timber-laden German ship brought into Yarmouth Harbour. It was one of the first prizes of war.'

The blow had fallen, but few had any idea how heavy it was to be. Most people said 'It'll all be over by Christmas'. J.T.B., who now held a teaching position at Ashford in Kent, returned for the autumn term to find the town full of Belgian refugees. They had fled before the German invader and had crossed the Straits of Dover in every kind of vessel, mostly fishing smacks. Ashford people turned a large shop and warehouse into a receiving centre and hostel, gave the refugees clothes, work and entertainments, and organized classes to teach them English.

Said J.T.B.: 'That was the beginning of my experience of relief work for war victims. I could not have believed that it was to continue on and off for more than thirty years. From that day, war or near-war has continued.'

The soldiers also came to Ashford, thousands of British soldiers in the last stages of training before crossing to France. One night J.T.B.'s class at an evening school was suddenly closed: the army had commandeered billets in the building. Two privates of the Northumberland Fusiliers, miners by trade, were billeted on the Baily home. Giving a hand with the washing-up, they joked about their future overseas.

'I expect I shan't be long before I'm kicking the daisies,' said one. It turned out to be true.

The Red-and-Black Star

The daisy-fields around Ashford became a final training ground for Tommy Atkins, where drill sergeants encouraged him to run forward with ferocious noises, and stick his bayonet into suspended sacks of straw. Then came the first black-out. The Zeppelins were caught in pencils of searchlight over Ashford. The war in the air that H. G. Wells had predicted was a reality. Bombs fell on Ashford; silly little bombs, a foot long, they dropped in a warren outside the town and killed one or two sheep.

By midsummer a year later the Germans were in occupation of Belgium and Northern France, the first gas attacks had been suffered at Ypres, the Allied armies were bogged-down in desperate defence of the Channel ports. Flanders had become a charnel-house for the young manhood of Europe.

'It was again my school vacation, but in common with others I decided that it was no time for holiday making. I offered my services to the Friends' War Victims Relief Committee which had been sending teams of workers over to Northern France, but I was not accepted because a Government regulation limited overseas relief workers to those who could promise not less than three months' service. Instead I was given a job in a big warehouse in London, off Ludgate Circus, unpacking and sorting gifts of clothing, footwear, and bedding, which came in from well-wishers, and packing it for shipment to France and other stricken countries.'

A red-and-black star was the emblem of the Friends' War Victims Relief work. It had first been worn in the Franco-Prussian War of 1870 when the English statesman John Bright and other Quakers had organized a relief fund and about forty volunteers had gone to the battlefields. During and after two world wars it has appeared on and behind the fighting fronts; the Quaker star on the vehicles and the dress of men and women who gave their services to suffering humanity is remembered in many parts of the world. This organization was known among its workers as 'the War Vics'. In addition many young Quakers joined the Friends' Ambulance Unit and went to the fronts manning hospital trains and motor ambulances. Others, as conscientious objectors, went to prison.

Craftsman and Quaker

Statesmen and generals were by 1915 resolved to a long war. With this prospect before him, J.T.B. had no taste for returning to school-mastering at the end of the summer vacation. One day while working in the Ludgate Circus warehouse he was called to the telephone to hear the familiar voice of Alfred Lynn, his old friend of the Adult School at St Albans: 'Hello, James, I'm speaking from St Stephen's House. We've been considering some distressing reports from our visitors to the internment camps. Your name was mentioned because of your technical qualifications. Will you come along to discuss things?'

St Stephen's House was the headquarters of another Quaker organization, the FEC—the Friends' Emergency Committee. The problem they were up against was the plight of thousands of civilian 'enemy aliens', mostly Germans and Austrians, who had been rounded-up and interned. Separated from their families and put behind barbed wire in camps hurriedly established up and down the country, the internees sat about in idleness, behind the barbed wire. They lacked the discipline of military prisoners of war; moreover, under the Geneva Convention civilian internees may not be ordered to work, whereas military prisoners can be. Idleness breeds moral and physical deterioration. The British military authorities who found themselves saddled with this unexpected incubus were quite willing when the FEC asked if they might send James T. Baily to investigate the trouble.

'I joined Robert Clark, a Quaker from British Columbia, on a visit to a camp at Lofthouse Park, near Wakefield. We found that a moral rot had set in. Immediate steps were taken by the Friends' Emergency Committee to provide books and magazines, woodworking tools and timber, and leatherworkers' and book-binders' equipment; tailors and shoemakers soon got busy with repairs, working for their fellows; even the most unskilled began to turn out simple objects such as blotter pads and writing-cases from scrap cardboard. It was remarkable how soon this organized (but voluntary) labour improved the morale and discipline of the prisoners. The things they made were sold to provide the men with a little money for their families, who had in most cases been left destitute.

The Red-and-Black Star

'One day when I passed a young sentry in khaki guarding the entrance to Lofthouse Park I was told that the man's father was interned inside the camp. The English-born soldier was guarding his German-born father.

'I went on to Handforth Camp, near Manchester, where a large dye-works had been requisitioned. I asked for any prisoners who were known to be craftsmen, with the intention of getting them to teach others. An officer took me to a hut where a little German rose from a table where he had been carving a box in white holly-wood.

' "This is very beautiful work," I said. "You must be a professional wood-carver."

' "No," he answered. "Until they brought me here I was in service in Scotland."

' "Service?"

' "I was a valet," he said.

'He was very shy, but when he saw my admiration of his work he began to thaw out.

' "I married a Scottish girl," he remarked.

'I asked him where he had obtained tools for such delicate carving as he was doing.

' "I made them," he replied.

'For a saw, he had serrated the back edge of a dinner knife with a file. For a hammer, he had salvaged an old lock, taken out the bolt, and seized it by means of wire to a piece of wood which he had shaped into a shaft. Various sizes and shapes of chisels he had made from broken bits of knife blades fitted into pieces of stick. Bradawls were fashioned from nails. From a small block of wood he had, with much patient labour, modelled a small plane.

'I obtained a proper set of tools for this Mr Wildmann. Later on, after he had been transferred to the Isle of Man, he continued to ply his skill under better organized conditions.'

The Quakers came in for abuse and criticism from press and public on account of this relief work among 'enemy aliens'—which is not surprising, for the hatred and distrust caused by war corrupt human relationships and vitiate the Christian virtues.

Craftsman and Quaker

Ironically, it was from the military authorities that the work received strongest approval: 'At Handforth Camp the commandant, a one-armed lieutenant-colonel of the regular army, gave me every facility to organize the men's work and to get tools and materials for them. Again, at Stobs Camp, close to Hawick in Scotland, where there were about 4,500 prisoners, the military commandant had the good of his charges very much at heart. Apart from any question of humanity, these commandants were quick to realize that idleness is bad for discipline, and is a breeding ground for grousing and misdemeanours.

'On arrival one day at Stobs I found the commandant in distress. "One of the chaps committed suicide during the night," he said. "As far as I can find out, he has been continuously teased by other men, and accused of having syphilis. He went to the hospital and was examined by the doctor who gave him an absolutely clean bill of health. But the teasing went on. Again he went to the hospital. This time, to humour him and hoping it would save him from further persecution, he was admitted, but his mind had become unstable and last night he hanged himself by his necktie."

'The commandant remarked about the influence of idle gossip on sensitive minds and asked me to impress it upon the prisoners whenever I had the opportunity.'

And so J.T.B. found himself in a totally unexpected position. The artisan was now in a true sense a missionary as well; the youth who had aspired to be an artisan-missionary in Africa found himself cast for a not unlike role in the prisoner-of-war camps. Besides being consulted on technical matters—workshops, tools, etc. on which he was expert—his help was sought on psychiatric issues to which he could bring only his common sense and his Christian penetration. He felt humbly inadequate for this, and yet he knew within a growing conviction that his life's experiences, from early days of roughing it in a working-class environment to his teaching behind bars at Borstal, had all been material melted in a crucible from which some essence could now be poured, something which he hoped by God's grace to give to suffering humanity; and if this service was at the same time of value to his country, as the camp commandants seemed to think, he was the happier, for J.T.B. found no relish in kicking against the pricks. When people pointed the finger of scorn at him and called him 'shirker' and even 'traitor' it hurt.

In wartime it is not easy to try to live according to the injunction to love your enemies, but the course of action taken by J.T.B. and other pacifists stemmed from their belief that war was utterly un-Christian: taking no part in the fighting, they felt a duty to succour the victims of war, of any and every nationality. At one period of the fighting in France the Friends' Ambulance Unit had temporarily to withdraw its men because French army officers were trying to prevent them from aiding the German as well as the Allied wounded. Similarly in the relief work in connection with prisoners of war and their dependants, the Quakers recognized no distinction of nationality. Many of the wives of prisoners were, in fact, British, and their children British-born, and thousands of these were given food, fuel, and medical attention during the war; and large numbers of the men had lived so long in this country as to have lost sympathy and contact with their land of birth. Others were, of course, dyed-in-the-wool Germans, and the mixture of the two types in captivity was another source of trouble.

Combatant prisoners of war were by 1915 coming in rapidly from the battle fronts. The War Office and Home Office decided to concentrate practically all civilian internees in the Isle of Man, vacating the other camps in England and Scotland to accommodate the military and naval prisoners. A huge hutment-city of some 25,000 inhabitants mushroomed behind barbed wire at Knockaloe on the west coast of the Isle of Man. The FEC asked J.T.B. to go there. He obtained leave of absence (unpaid) from the Kent Education Committee, to the end of 1915. This meant living on the nominal salary of a Quaker relief worker, supplemented by his savings; but he regarded himself as fortunate compared with the prisoners, most of whom had no income at all, and to all of whom the journey to the Isle of Man must have seemed like banishment to Siberia. The delectable holiday-isle in the Irish Sea lost its charms when seen through barbed-wire in mid-winter.

'I was at Handforth Camp arranging the transfer of our equipment to the Isle of Man when relatives and friends were visiting the men for the last time before their removal. One poor woman came past me vainly striving to check her tears as she left her husband, realising that there would be little chance of seeing him again until the war was over. A young woman walked away with a tiny babe pressed to her breast, daring not to look back at the husband to whom she had just said goodbye. The scene was tragic as the women and children met the prisoners and said farewell.'

Not long after this J.T.B. passed through London Road Station at Manchester, and his diary records: 'Witnessed a pathetic scene, the departure of soldiers returning to the front, amid a crowd of weeping women and children. Oh God, how long is this awful tragedy to continue?'

His first voyage to the Isle of Man was in a dense fog. The ship groped its way across the Irish Sea, with monotonous blasts on its siren. Then the mist cleared and a dim blue smudge on the horizon became the magnificent sweep of Douglas Bay, with Onchan Head at the northern end and Douglas Head at the south. The hotels, boarding houses, and places of entertainment along the promenade of the 'playground of Lancashire' were vacant and boarded-up. War had put a stop to the holiday-making habits of northcountry folk; German submarines lurked in the Irish Sea, and the cross-channel boats from Liverpool were laden with dismal internees.

'I boarded a railway train to cross the island to the small fishing port of Peel. The Isle of Man Railway, with its narrow-gauge tracks, its ancient engines and old-fashioned carriages, has often been the object of jokes, and on one occasion I remember seeing these words which someone had written in large letters under the luggage rack:

PASSENGERS ARE REQUESTED NOT TO PLUCK THE
FLOWERS WHILE THE TRAIN IS IN MOTION

The Red-and-Black Star

but on this occasion as I looked out of the windows I was glad of our sedate progress, for there was much to admire—flowers colouring the hedgerows and carpeting the railway cuttings, mountains purple with heather and golden with gorse. I realized that this little island in the Irish Sea is a very lovely place.

'The same thought was with me as I walked the two miles from Peel along a country road to the camp. Then I saw Knockaloe: rows and rows of the black roofs and the brown wooden sides of army huts, miles and miles of sleeper-tracks between them. I crossed a bridge over a small river which tinkled between leafy banks, winding its easy way to the sea. Seagulls flew inland from the nearby port of Peel, where an ancient and romantic castle looks down upon the fishing craft in the harbour.

'The Isle of Man was a romantic and historic land, full of beauty, until you came to Knockaloe.'

At the main gates of the camp sentries stood with fixed bayonets. J.T.B. presented his credentials, and was taken to the commandant, a grey-haired veteran of the South African War. The colonel had the familiar unsavoury tale to tell, of the sexual perversities of an all-male society, of the mischief of idle minds and hands, and of 'barbed-wire disease': the symptoms of this were moroseness, avoidance of others, and an aimless promenading up and down the barbed-wire boundary of the compound, like a wild animal in a cage. The consequence might be insanity, perhaps suicide. Later, J.T.B. was told by Swiss and Swedish Government attachés, when they visited the Isle of Man, that 'barbed-wire disease' was common in all concentration camps of the belligerents. The surest way to prevent and to cure it while the war continued was to banish idleness. To this task the Friends' relief services gave their attention.

Tools and timber were shipped to Knockaloe. A few men started to work, and then more and more. First they took the opportunity to improve their living quarters and to make equipment for games, libraries, and gardening, to rig up camp theatres, etc. Then small articles of woodwork were made for sale outside the camp, and later this developed into a fairly large-scale production of toys and light furniture, with sales in Great Britain and Ireland, the USA, Sweden, Holland, and Denmark.

The effect of this work on morale was emphatic: where demoralisation and 'barbed-wire disease' continued it was usually among those men who stubbornly or lazily refused to engage in any activity.

There was a similar situation in Germany, where 4,000 British civilians were interned in the racecourse buildings at Ruhleben, near Berlin. Among them was Sir Timothy Eden, Bart. (brother of Mr Anthony Eden), who on his release from this camp in 1916 wrote a letter to the London *Times* urging the belligerents to make a straight exchange of all their civilian prisoners, for humanitarian reasons. The Britishers in Ruhleben, he wrote, were travellers or residents in Germany in 1914 who 'were arrested and clapped into concentration camps where they have remained ever since, ignored or forgotten by the majority of Englishmen at home. . . . I cannot lay too much stress upon the serious mental condition of the civilian prisoners. And this condition is only natural. Suddenly snatched from their peaceful occupations, these men have been herded into a racecourse, where they have now lived in crowded stables for two years. For not a single instant during the whole of that time has any prisoner had the slightest privacy.'[1]

There were humanitarians in Germany who went into Ruhleben camp to help, members of the pre-war Anglo-German Friendship movement. Their secretary, Dr Elizabeth Rotten, had been a university lecturer at Cambridge. The Society of Friends in London was able to keep in touch with these German relief workers through the neutral embassies, and many troublesome knots between prisoners and their relatives on either side of the battlefront were thus unravelled. A public appeal issued in Berlin in 1914 is remarkably similar in spirit to the line taken by the Quakers in Britain: 'Even in wartime whoever needs our help is our neighbour. A love of their enemies remains the distinguishing mark of those who are loyal to our Lord.'

[1] *The Times*, November 22nd, 1916.

The Red-and-Black Star

Between such an ethic and its translation into action lay a host of difficulties. At Knockaloe in the Isle of Man the sheer size of the camp (as large as Salisbury or Chelmsford) must have made J.T.B.'s job seem at first almost impossible; and as thousands of prisoners came over from England and were dumped on the bleak Manx hillside their harassed military guardians, saddled with unfamiliar situations, did not invariably welcome the Englishman with the red-and-black star in his buttonhole.

J.T.B. had obtained a government pass into the camp, but few of the officers of the guard had heard of the work of FEC in the camps on the mainland and at first they resented the intrusion of a Quaker pacifist in civvies. Some gave him a frigid reception. They marked him down as 'pro-German' and 'unpatriotic'. One officer said: 'If I had my way I would put you and your like up against a wall and shoot you.'

On his first Sunday in the Isle of Man J.T.B. climbed to the top of Peel Hill. It was a glorious day of bright sunshine, with a sharp snap in the air. He sat on a mass of springy heather and looked down on the little port of Peel, its streets and quays very quiet on the Sabbath morning. Red sandstone cliffs stretched away by the sea which shimmered in the shining splendour of the sun. Inland, the gorse-covered hills of Man ranged as far as the eye could see.

'As I looked upon them I saw the one thing in that pleasing prospect that saddened me, the dark square patch on the distant hillside of Knockaloe, the camp where 23,000 non-combatant victims of the war were living, the duration of their detention unpredictable. As I mused thus, my thoughts turned to my own loved ones, at this moment gathered with Ashford Friends in meeting for worship. In spirit I was drawn to worship with them, though I was seemingly alone on that hilltop. I had a wonderful sense of the Divine presence and of unity with those so far away. Thus I remained throughout an hour, feeling thanksgiving for the ministration of nature's beauty around me, and pondering upon the immensity of the task awaiting me in that black prison town.'

After J.T.B. had sized up the situation and discussed it with the

Craftsman and Quaker

camp commandant, Lieutenant-Colonel Panzera, the FEC in London appointed him its permanent representative at Knockaloe, with the title Industrial Adviser. A Quaker hut was erected just outside the main gates of the camp, as a stores and office.

Then Horatio Bottomley went into action. The editor of *John Bull* had a fancy for alliterative headlines, and this one signalised the breaking of the storm:

TEACHING TREACHEROUS TEUTONS

A violent attack on J.T.B. and his work, and on the government for allowing it to be done, was written in Bottomley's best hymn-of-hate style. It gave copy to other papers all over the country. At Ashford the local journal described him as 'Kent Teacher for Hun Prisoners'. His wife had to put up with all kinds of offensiveness. Whenever she took a parcel to the post office to be despatched to the Isle of Man, it was passed along the counter for all to see and to make facetious remarks. Angry citizens, members of the local education sub-committee, passed a resolution calling on the Kent Education Committee to dismiss James T. Baily. The Director of Education for the county reminded them that only a few months previously they had granted Baily leave of absence to the end of the war. He refused to put the recommendation forward because to do so was irregular and would give Baily the right to take action for wrongful dismissal. There the matter had to remain.

Soon after being pilloried by Horatio Bottomley, J.T.B. was summoned to appear as a conscientious objector before a tribunal. Conscription had come into force; his age-group was due for call-up. What mental and spiritual agonies of reappraisal this meant no one can say. He knew full well that many Christians took the view, very sincerely, that they had to fight the evil of Prussianism with the weapons that the Germans themselves were using. He had no wish to shelter behind the sacrifice of others. He re-examined the Quaker testimony against war. As far back as 1660 they had addressed their conviction to King Charles II:

Sibford School in Oxfordshire, the scene of an experiment in the teaching of crafts. This part of the school is the old Manor House of Sibford Ferris.

The woodwork shop. The teacher is Roland Herbert.

13

The Quaker Star in Vienna, 1919

The famine in Germany after the first world war. Distributing 'Quaker' soup in Berlin

The Red-and-Black Star

'We utterly deny all outward wars and strife, and fightings with outward weapons, for any end, or under any pretence whatever; this is our testimony to the whole world.'

Between that declaration and 'Your King and Country need you' lay the hateful choice.

He made his decision. He could not break the Quaker testimony against war without shattering his own sense of Christian values: 'I could do no other. If I could not fight I could at least try to help clear up the mess.' But even this last choice—willingness to accept what the government called 'alternative service' in ambulance or relief work—entailed some heart-burning: there were pacifists, including some of J.T.B.'s dearest Quaker friends, who held that to accept the direction of a tribunal to alternative service prejudiced the total and traditional testimony against war because it was a tacit acceptance of the Military Service Act, to which they were opposed as something that outraged the conscience of man. J.T.B. could follow the logic of this, but it was not his way. He went, nevertheless, to the tribunal prepared to argue a Christian pacifist case. He was astonished to hear his name read out as 'exempted from military service because engaged in work of national importance'.

At the end of the tribunal he asked the clerk why his case had not been heard. The clerk replied curtly: 'The case has been decided and is closed.'

Lieutenant-Colonel Panzera had sent a personal letter to the tribunal requesting James T. Baily's retention in the camp service, and stating that in the interests of discipline his work was essential. When J.T.B. learned of this he wrote: 'I would rather have had an opportunity to state my case on religious grounds, much as I appreciated the commandant's evaluation of my work.'

He was then forty years of age.

VIII

The Malignant City

Comedy and tragedy were in partnership at Knockaloe. Incarceration produces its own wry humour. There was the cheery spirit who wrote verses for a camp revue, produced during the worst period of the First World War's food shortage:

> Last week a pal of mine invited me to tea—
> 'I've got a real good joint,' he said.
> Of course I went with glee.
> And sure enough the meat was there,
> It was no blooming lark,
> But when I put my fork in it
> The joint began to bark!

Such humour is surely more English in idiom than German. 'And there was more than a grain of truth in it,' said J.T.B. 'I knew one prisoner whose pet dog mysteriously vanished. A few hours later they were eating an excellent dinner of "rabbit" in the next compound.'

Sometimes comedy and tragedy joined hands. There was the day when an orderly tapped on the Quaker hut door: 'Major Quayle-Dickson's compliments, sir, and will you see him at his office as early as convenient, please?' J.T.B. walked along the sleeper track to the sub-commandant's office of Camp 3. (Knockaloe was divided for administrative purposes into four sections of some five to six thousand men.)

'Good day, Baily,' said Major Quayle-Dickson. 'Glad you were able to come up. Case of a bereavement. The man's elderly and the loss of his wife will be a big blow to him. He's worried about his family's welfare. Can you help?'

The Malignant City

The major handed over a telegram, issued from a north-east England town: 'Mother passed away this morning, Mary.'

The prisoner was summoned. J.T.B. spoke to him privately and promised to get members of the Society of Friends in his home town to attend the needs of his family.

A few days later when J.T.B. paid a routine visit to Camp 3 the sub-commandant was waiting on the doorstep of his hut, a grin on his face and a letter held in his hand.

'Just look at this, Baily! You remember last Saturday's case?'

'The man whose wife died?'

'She's not dead. This letter came for him this morning.'

My dear husband,

I am very sorry you are so upset, it is not I who am dead but my mother.

I did think you would have recognised my handwriting on the telegram.

The confusion had been caused by the fact that the prisoner's wife and daughter both had the name of Mary. He had jumped to the conclusion that his wife was dead when it was really his mother-in-law.

Knockaloe was the strangest city in history. It had no women and no children. Its industries were initiated from outside for humanitarian reasons, yet they developed into a vital part of its social structure and were the salvation of many of its inhabitants, but when peace came they all vanished. And the city that had been built of fifteen million feet of timber and a million bricks, surrounded by seven hundred miles of barbed wire, all disappeared at the war's end, and today the plough tills the land where was once a prison. All that is left is in the graveyard of the little Manx church nearby: the long rows of stones for Germans, Austrians, Hungarians, Bulgarians, and Turks who died in this foreign land.

As the months lengthened into years the prisoners sorted out their own civilization: there were theatres, there were camp

Craftsman and Quaker

orchestras with players whose names had been well known in pre-war London, there were football leagues and tennis matches, there were classes of every description from art to political economy. And there were the industries, fostered by J.T.B.

Improvisation played a large part, as it must when imprisoned men pit their ingenuity and fingers against inadequacy of materials and tools. There was an acute shortage of sheet metal, but there was no shortage of empty bully-beef tins. These were cut up, flattened into sheets, made into mugs, cake tins, baking pans, pastry cutters, funnels, scoops, boxes, candlesticks, ashtrays, footlights, and suits of armour for theatrical productions.

At first the huts where the men lived had no water-gutterings; rain-water falling on the compounds was drained away in open trenches. These gulleys were dangerous during hours of darkness, until an inventive prisoner suggested that if you knock the top and bottom out of a bully-beef tin the remaining part with its slightly sloping sides can be telescoped into others similarly treated, thereby providing lines of drain-pipes. These were laid, the trenches were filled in, and civilization advanced a step further.

Imprisoned sculptors, for want of better material, carved the meat-bones discarded by the cook-houses. The bones were first boiled to remove fat, marrow, and gristle, then bleached with soda or bleaching powder. Long leg bones were transfigured into slender flower vases decorated with carvings of roses, tulips, lilies, or a human figure. The shorter bones were made into pincushions, ashtrays, match and cigarette stands, table cructs, napkin rings, paper knives, and brooches, very delicately carved. This became a big industry; Manx POW bonework found its way to buyers all over the world. The most exquisite pieces were carved by one of the brothers Lang of Oberammergau Passion Play fame.

German inventiveness was on its mettle. One man invented a machine for making tooth-brush handles from the old bones. Another prisoner, named Holzsinger, acquired an ancient sock-knitting machine and advertised in the camp that if anyone would

The Malignant City

deliver to him three pairs of old socks he would reproduce from them one good pair at a small charge. He devised a means of unwinding the wool of the socks and using it on his knitting machine to make the new pair. This venture was so successful that soon Holzsinger was able to employ others and to add more machines, which J.T.B. obtained.

'His hut became a knitting workshop, and was kept busy. There was a sequel to this sock-knitting enterprise in 1920, when I visited Germany. Among a group of ex-prisoners who met me at the station at Hamburg was Herr Holzsinger, who invited me to visit his new knitting factory. He had put the knowledge and experience acquired at Knockaloe to good purpose. And his business notepaper, I noticed, carried as a trade mark the three legs of Man!

'In a rather similar way the tailors of Knockaloe did a brisk business in remaking suits and overcoats, taking them carefully to pieces and turning the cloth inside out. Some very smart wear was produced, as many of the cutters and tailors had worked with first-class outfitters in peacetime.'

The diary left by J.T.B. is punctuated with set-backs as well as triumphs:

'Saw a bookbinder and got arrangements in hand for starting book-binding department. Then to Compound 5 to pass woodwork and carved bonework for despatch to USA. Had some trouble with some of the workers over inferior work. . . . Cable arrived today for 4,000 dollars-worth of goods for the USA.'

And again:

'Two members of Theatre Committee conferred with me, feeling aggrieved that Industrial Committee is charging them too much for theatre fittings. One result of internment is that men get very suspicious; they listen to and believe in every bit of tittle-tattle they hear, and become jealous of any little authority they acquire in the camp. . . .'

Craftsman and Quaker

Woodworking and carving were the most widely practised of the crafts; in the workshops the men were always busy and a large number of amateurs learned something of woodworking during their internment. A craftsman, Charles Matt, who before the war had been foreman in charge of about eighty men in a London furniture factory, gathered round him some of the finest professional cabinet-makers, and the authorities allowed a couple of huts to be allocated to them. Here was made some remarkable furniture, designed on what was then 'modernist' lines, for Mr W. J. Bassett-Lowke, the engineering model-maker of Northampton. An ardent supporter of the modern movement in design—he was one of the leaders in the formation of the Design in Industries Association—Bassett-Lowke had built at Northampton a revolutionary house which he called 'New Ways'; with its flat roof and simple surfaces, it was the first 'modern' house to be built in England, and it was furnished with the beautiful Knockaloe furniture of Charles Matt and his colleagues, made to the designs of the world-famous architect of 'New Ways', Charles Mackintosh. To have a part in such work delighted the craftsman in J.T.B. To see so many untutored amateurs find an unknown craft at their finger-tips confirmed his peacetime experience in schools, that craft-ability is natural to more people than realize it.

But sadness was inseparable from work in an internment camp: 'How often did I hear this sort of thing: "Mr Baily, just think, my son was six when I was arrested, now he is ten and I shall hardly know him. I wonder if he will remember me. And to think all these years are passing and I have no part in his life and upbringing." '

Ninety-eight men were tried by military courts for attempting to escape from Knockaloe during the war. Not one succeeded in getting away from the Isle of Man. Two German sailors came near to it, but their adventure ended in tragi-comedy. One dark night they cut their way through the barbed wire and walked to Peel harbour, where a number of fishing boats were moored. They clambered down into one, quietly got the sails ready, and cast off the mooring rope, only to find that the boat was firmly

The Malignant City

aground. The tide was out in that part of the harbour. They transferred everything to another boat which was afloat, and were about to slip out to sea when a fisherman taking a late stroll on the opposite side of the harbour heard a noise and called to them. Getting no reply, he raised an alarm. An armed sentry at the harbour mouth covered the boat with his rifle until police arrived and the two men surrendered.

They had maps and a compass on them. These must have been smuggled into Knockaloe under the nose of the censor's department. Every day three or four cartloads of mail-bags and parcels passed in and out of the camp, and attempts to delude the censor were frequent. Forbidden articles and messages were found inside cakes, and even inside walnuts. Boxes with false bottoms and books with secret hiding-places were common tricks. Codes worked into the ornamental borders of garments put British intelligence officers on their mettle. One censor was posted in the Quaker hut to check parcels of materials coming in and finished goods going out.

The seas around the Isle of Man were a favourite hunting-ground for German submarines. The Isle of Man steam packets were never attacked. When J.T.B. visited Germany after the war he was told on high authority that the U-boat captains had orders not to molest these steamers because they frequently carried German prisoners. But many other ships bound in and out of Liverpool and Belfast were torpedoed, including the White Star liner *Celtic*. With two gaping holes in her sides, she was successfully beached off Peel in March, 1918, her decks awash. Survivors were rushed ashore and the ship's cargo and coal were taken off to lighten her. The Knockaloe food contractor bought a few cheap lines in jettisoned victuals, so there was a change of diet in the camp mess, 'but the turkey was more or less high', says J.T.B.'s diary. Divers patched the *Celtic's* hull and she was towed to Belfast for dry-dock repairs.

By 1918 the range of industrial activities under J.T.B.'s supervision in Knockaloe was very wide, from printing to gardening. The authorities now felt that his position should be made

Craftsman and Quaker

more 'official' and he was transferred to the Manx government service.

'My title was changed from Industrial Advisor to Industrial Superintendent, but my work remained much the same.'

Nearly 65,000 baskets were manufactured in the camp, using willow grown in the Isle of Man, and this almost led to the foundation of a new Manx industry as a permanency after the war. Its story of success and failure is worth telling in case some enterprising Manxman may yet spring to the opportunity. It all began by the accident that there were four professional basket-makers interned in Camp 3. J.T.B. got materials from England, and encouraged the four to act as instructors to others. Eventually eighty men became skilled at this craft, and special huts were allocated for it. Major Quayle-Dickson, as a Manxman himself, began to think that it would be a pity to see this new industry vanish with the end of the war, for the Isle of Man was badly in need of permanent industries to balance the seasonal holiday traffic, its main source of trade in peacetime.

At first J.T.B. had bought supplies of willows from Lancashire and Nottinghamshire: 'But it seemed wasteful to import from England when there were areas of the Isle of Man which appeared at first sight to be natural willow-growing lands. I gathered samples of wild sallows from the banks of the River Neb near Knockaloe, and some from the Curragh, an extensive flat area at the northern end of the island, and I asked our four basket-making leaders to give me their opinion on the material. They rejected it as useless, which was only to be expected from craftsmen accustomed to the best-grown osiers, but I persuaded them to try the stuff out, giving as a reason the well-worn argument that "there's a war on". The four craftsman experimented and produced some excellent baskets and hampers.

'Major Quayle-Dickson and I could now see big possibilities ahead. One day we went to the Curragh with the Rector of Ballaugh and others who were interested, to examine the possibility of extensive willow-growing there. All day we explored this area, arriving very hungry for tea at Ballaugh Rectory, not

The Malignant City

having had a meal since an early breakfast. The immediate result of the day was that the Curragh land-owners who tramped with us agreed that if we would get prisoners of war to clear the ground of the sallow willows, we could take away all we wanted; this was on December 11, 1917, a fine frosty day.

'I made a report to the Manx Government Secretary, and sought his advice. He issued a wartime order commandeering all willow-growths on the island, and giving me power to take prisoners in working parties anywhere, to cut and transport the osiers to Knockaloe. These parties went out under a military escort, taking rations with them for the day. It was a very pleasant interlude for the men; they coveted the outings as a privilege, and only once was the privilege abused, if that is the right word to use. On December 24, 1917, I took a working party to Sulby Glen, but little was done, they were more intent on gathering evergreen decorations for their huts in the camp. Like Nelson, I had to turn a blind eye, it being Christmas Eve.

'A Douglas merchant offered to buy all the baskets we could make, for export to England. Potato, vegetable, and fruit hampers were at that time in very short supply in England and we soon had orders for laundry hampers, wicker suitcases, lounge chairs, clothes baskets, and we even made a wicker side-car for a motor-cycle.

'Thinking of post-war possibilities, a far-seeing Manxman, Mr Copeland Smith, formed Manx Industries Ltd. I sought specialist opinion, and Mr Hutchinson of the Department of Agriculture and Fisheries in London, an authority on osier cultivation, came to the Isle of Man; he and I went over the ground together. The Curragh alone, he reported, could be made to provide not only sufficient osiers for a large industry in the island but also for export to the mainland. There were other potentially productive areas near Port St Mary and Peel.

'Consideration of the scheme dragged on month after month after the end of the war, then the Government Secretary had to confess that the difficulties facing the taking over of the Curragh were seemingly insuperable owing to vested interests in the land.

Craftsman and Quaker

Manx Industries languished and died, and Mr Copeland Smith left the island for the USA. One of my few regrets at coming back to England from the Isle of Man after the war was to leave this dream unaccomplished.'

At the armistice 24,450 men were in Knockaloe. Only sixteen per cent of these were permitted to take up residence again in Britain. It took nearly a year to send the others back to the lands of their birth. J.T.B. remained in the Isle of Man during this twilight of the malignant city.

'This was in many ways the worst period of all. The winter of 1918–19 was a particularly bad one, with stormy weather, drenching cold rains, and an influenza epidemic to add to the depression which fell upon the men as their release was delayed. It was uphill work trying to keep them occupied and interested as the months dragged by. They were listless and restless, gloomy and bitter. A government tribunal which considered the appeals of those who desired to remain in Britain was turning most of them down. When they were deported some of their wives refused to leave this country, and this led to separations and divorce. At Knockaloe during these months the industries languished; promises to undertake and finish jobs were continually broken; time and time again our efforts to have final stocktakings and to wind-up industrial affairs were exasperatingly delayed.

'One morning in October 1919, I stood at the camp gate and watched the last 175 march out under escort, down the road to Peel, en route to freedom—a mixed crowd, old and young, some gay, some morose. At the bend of the road a few turned and waved their caps, then they were lost to sight.

'To what were they going? Liberty? Reunion? Food and clothing in plenty? Everlasting peace? Justice and toleration?

'Alone, I walked for the last time up the wooden sleeper-track between the empty huts. Two things I noticed. A dog was vainly rushing through the huts looking for human companions. And in the centre of an open compound where for five years men had walked and idled, played football, and waited under the Manx skies, a sickly looking plant in a pot was standing in the

The Malignant City

middle of the barrack square of trodden cinders. It had been placed there by a prisoner, his last thought before leaving.'

When J.T.B. came back to England after four years at Knockaloe he received a letter from the Lieutenant-Governor of the Isle of Man expressing thanks for the work—'resulting as it did in the manufacture of many thousands of articles for the making of which British labour was not available'.

His Excellency was pleased to add that 'you may reflect upon your work during the war as having been of no small value to the country'.

It was an unexpected end to the period of 'teaching treacherous Teutons'.

IX

Mission of Peace

He did not return to teaching. Not yet, anyhow. Half of Europe had collapsed into famine, anarchy, and starvation. Letters were coming back to J.T.B. from ex-Knockaloe men, telling of the terrible things that were happening in Germany. Quaker relief teams were working desperately across Europe, from revolution-torn Russia to liberated France. When the Society of Friends asked J.T.B. if he would join their famine-relief workers in Germany, to tour the country and report on conditions, he accepted at once. Through an ex-prisoners' association he was able to meet many men who had been sent back from England, and to see how they were settling down, and in this way it came about that he addressed over thirty large meetings in Germany. He obtained a unique close-up of a defeated nation at a time when official relationships between victors and vanquished were icy and 'fraternization' was definitely forbidden for our army of occupation.

It was a strange thing that an Englishman should thus meet large numbers of the German people on an intimate footing within a few months of their bitter defeat, and yet should appear not as a renegade Englishman (his visit had the approval of the British Government); anything less like a fellow-traveller of defeated Prussianism or nascent Hitlerism than J.T.B. would be difficult to imagine, but it was only to be expected that people on both sides, victors and defeated, should find it hard at a time of inflated war passions to understand the Quaker 'line'. As J.T.B. put it:

'The first-aid aspect of our relief work, whether it was helping men in the prisoner-of-war camps or feeding starving children in Europe, was not the whole of our attitude; it was only one practical consequence of Quaker pacifist beliefs. Behind such activities lies a philosophy which is as sternly opposed to aggression as that of any general or admiral or prime minister, but which cannot agree with opposing force by force. To us the rape of Belgium in 1914 by Prussian militarism was a monstrous crime, as were the later Nazi, Fascist, and Communist aggressions, and we continually said so. But the evil does not begin with an aggression; it begins with the baleful effect of militarism on the actions and policy of all nations, ours and others, with the piling up of armaments, and the fear, distrust, and war mentality which always goes with it. These things tend to produce war, not to prevent it. We believe that the only other way is by the Christian doctrine of love, in peacetime or in wartime.

'In Germany after the First World War I saw among the people a disgust with militarism, a waiting for high-minded leadership by European and American statesmen. Unhappily, they were not high-minded enough and the Germans were led away into evil by Adolf Hitler.'

In the between-the-wars years J.T.B. was an admirer of Gandhi's method of passive resistance to aggression, though he failed to appreciate Gandhi's subtle political skill. There was no politician in J.T.B. He saw in simple terms what he conceived to be his Christian duty, and he tried to do it. He was at his happiest when carrying it out in some really practical way.

One of the best examples of Quaker methods of practical reconciliation came when the German armies went into retreat and a 'War Vics' team took over responsibility for the rehabilitation of a large devastated area of France. Wooden prefabricated houses were supplied for the homeless, and *furniture was made for the French people by their 'enemies' in the Isle of Man.*

When the urgent need for this furniture was reported to J.T.B. at Knockaloe, he and Charles Matt prepared designs to suit the tools and material available in the prison camp, but at this period there was an acute shortage of timber: 'I had to search the island for it. At Ramsey I found a small yacht-builder's yard where the owner was disposing of his stock. Then I heard that some trees had been felled and were lying about in the fields towards

Craftsman and Quaker

Foxdale. So it came about that farms and cottages in France were furnished with tables, cupboards, and sideboards fashioned by German and Austrian prisoners of war, and made from Manx wood. Some of the Knockaloe tailors made clothing for little boys in northern France, and their boots and shoes were also made in our camp workshops. The design of the furniture was unusual: it all folded flat, to take up the minimum cargo space. The Friends' relief services chartered a small cargo steamer which loaded the furniture, clothing and boots at Peel and carried them directly to a French port.'

The following report came later from one of the Quaker workers in France:

> Mission de la Société des Amis,
> Grange le Comte,
>   Par Clermond en Argonne,
>   Meuse.
> le 4th January, 1920.

I recently made a visit to the villages where our relief workers have been distributing the furniture made by the Germans in the Isle of Man. I have been wishing that your committee might know how much this gift has been appreciated by the families who have received it.

It has been extremely difficult to procure any furniture here in France and that which we could succeed in buying was of a quite inferior quality, especially so as compared with the strong well-made pieces which came from the Isle of Man. The cupboards were given to families of six persons or over, the buffets to families of four or five persons, and the tables to families of less than four persons.

The schools in two of the villages were able to open sooner because of the Isle of Man tables, which were loaned until they could secure proper desks. All the furniture has been distributed to those villages of the Aisne where the families have suffered the hardships of two evacuations. In several of the little baraquements the piece of Isle of Man furniture was quite conspicuous as the

Mission of Peace

first substantial contribution towards the furnishing of a new home, and in every case the people were wonderfully appreciative and expressed their gratitude in the charming manner which the French people employ so gracefully.

We made it known to the French recipients by whom the furniture had been made and under what circumstances, and while I cannot report a great awakening of international interest they at least realized that war brought hardships and trials to all in one way and another.

Edith Collins Moon,
Sous-chef of relief.

From this it will be seen how the Quakers put their faith in the scattering of bread on the waters, however rough the current might be. To hope that somewhere in France, in Germany, in England, a hardened heart might be softened, that pity might begin to drive out revenge, and charity replace anger—these brave beliefs energised many activities, from feeding the starving to J.T.B.'s 1920 visit to Germany.

It was a war-weary nation he came to, a Germany occupied up to the Rhine by British, French, Belgian, and American troops, and beyond that uneasily ruled by a republican government which was unpopular with the extremists (who were to become the Nazis) for having signed the treaty of peace at Versailles. A blockade, continued by the Allies long after hostilities ended, was inflaming hatred and causing grievous suffering. During J.T.B.'s stay in Germany he himself lost two stones in weight.

He travelled with Charles Weiss, a Quaker who spoke good German. On the way out, at Amsterdam, they bought a large Dutch cheese. This went into their rucksack as iron rations.

'It was a shameful situation for us during the next few days to come down to meals in German hotels and see people having their meagre food and ersatz coffee. We had not the heart to place our cheese on the table; we surreptitiously broke off pieces inside the rucksack.

'At Hanover I addressed my first meeting of 350 ex-prisoners, their wives, and friends. I told them of the Society of Friends' work, its testimony for peace, and its opposition to militarism, pleading for German unity with us in rebuilding a state of life in Europe founded on love and not on fear. Charles Weiss translated for me. There followed a busy time attending to personal enquiries about property left behind or confiscated in England, and answering the pathetic questions from the English-born wives about chances of ever returning to England.'

Privately, J.T.B. was angry that the British government considered it lawful to confiscate all property and belongings in Britain of ex-prisoners as part-payment of the war indemnity payable by enemy countries; enemy governments were supposed to be liable to refund the losses to their returned nationals, but of course it did not often work out that way, and the sentimental losses were as grievous as the monetary value of the goods taken; worst of all, how could Europe hope to win the peace if a wartime mentality was to be perpetuated by such actions?

'At Elberfeld an ex-Knockaloe man invited me to tea at his house. His wife broke into tears as she told me how their household furniture was to be sold by the Public Trustee in London. One realized how, after years of home-making, the things of the home mean almost everything to the housewife. Sentiment counts for a lot in life—but this of course is not the sort of sentiment that appeals to politicians drawing up the reparation requirements in peace treaties.'

These were the thoughts of the relief workers in Germany. They kept them to themselves, and got on with the job. 'We reported to Quaker Relief HQ in Berlin concerning famine conditions so that action might be taken. In Hanover I noted the anaemic condition of women and children, and the looks of despair as they glanced at the windows of food shops, some boarded up, some marked with impossible inflationist prices. It is difficult to indicate the value of German money during this inflationary period. It was fluctuating wildly day by day, and in different parts of the country. During my visit some typical shop prices at the then rate of exchange were: boots, £10 a pair; suits, £60

14

Ackworth School in Yorkshire, where J. T. B was a master from 1923–37

Teaching in the Crafts Department he created.

<small>*Illustrations by courtesy of Ackworth School and the Yorkshire Evening Post*</small>

15

The old gymnasium at Ackworth and (below) *the metalwork shop into which it was transformed*

Mission of Peace

to £200; shirt, £3 10s 0d; a pram, £45. The average weekly cost of food for a typical working-class family had been 65 marks (£3 5s 0d) before the war; it was now 570 marks (£28 10s 0d).

'In town after town there was a heavy death-rate among children. At Leipzig I saw the American Quakers, under the organization of Herbert Hoover, giving a midday meal to undernourished children, which meant one-third of all the city's children. Throughout Germany the Americans were feeding 680,000 children every day.

'At Nuremberg and Munich supplies were not arriving from the countryside and there was great anxiety concerning diminishing food stocks, particularly of bread. At Nuremberg I wrote in my diary:

'Sat. March 13, 1920. I have had today the most awful of experiences, not of this visit but of my life, seeing starved babies and diseased and crippled children, the result of the war and the ensuing blockade. Both Charles and I felt quite ill and I had finally to request the doctor to refrain from showing us more.

'Stadtsekretar Hoffmann took us to see the Stadt Kinderheim where fifty-five orphaned schoolchildren are housed in what was formerly an infirmary for old people. Clothing and boots are in an awful condition. The matron, who looked half-starved herself, is getting desperate because the clothing has reached that final stage where washing renders it unmendable, and all the mending material she is able to get is some worn-out army pillow cases. She cannot get cotton, which costs the equivalent of twenty to thirty shillings per reel. The children are so weak as to be incapable of controlling their urinary organs; the wetted beds cannot be changed, and there are no waterproof sheets available.

'We also visited an infant hospital. It was too horrible; one felt as though an accusing finger was being pointed at oneself as an Englishman whose country retained the blockade of Germany for so long after the termination of hostilities. Babies were mere tiny skeletons covered with skin.

Craftsman and Quaker

'At Frankfurt-on-Main bread tickets were printed by the German authorities as permits for the receipt of relief. On the ticket was the figure of an old-fashioned Quaker Oats type of Quaker, and the words: Dank für die Quakerhilfe (Thanks for the Quaker-help).

'At Essen a schoolteacher told us she had asked her class the question "What is Paradise?" A little girl answered: "A place where there is always plenty to eat."

'This teacher went on to ask us what was "behind" the Quaker activities. We told her of our attitude, emphasizing that it was not pro-German but anti-war.'

So they cast their bread of peace upon the waters, and sometimes they found it after many days: 'At Halle I met Herr Rennemann who had been head captain of Compound 2, Camp 1, Knockaloe, and we had a long talk during which he admitted that before the war he had been a whole-hearted anti-British Prussian militarist. We had become good friends during his internment, and now he told me that his views were undergoing a change and that he had been much influenced by Quaker service during and after the war.'

One wonders what became of such converts from militarism later, under the Germany of the swastika and the concentration camps.

In England immediately the 1914–18 war was over politicians had been shouting on the hustings that we should 'squeeze Germany until the pips squeak' and the less responsible newspapers were playing to the gallery with the same hymn of revenge. In Germany, oddly enough, the Quakers found that the Britishers nearest to their own outlook were the soldiers of our army of occupation, who stood not very long at the barriers of hatred. Or was this odd? It was simply another proof that many hatreds are artificial and break down under human contact.

Non-fraternisation orders proved ineffective. During the interminable wranglings of the Versailles Peace Conference, Mr Lloyd George read a telegram in which General Plumer, Commander of the British Army of Occupation, said that a bad effect was

Mission of Peace

being produced on the British soldier's discipline by the spectacle of the sufferings of German women and children. The consequence of this incident was an agreement by the Allies to lift the blockade and send food into Germany on condition that it be paid for immediately in gold and that the German merchant fleet be surrendered forthwith.

'Unnecessary bitterness was caused by some of the actions of the Allies,' wrote J.T.B. 'While I was at Frankfurt a force of Senegalese troops were marched into the city to reinforce the French army of occupation. Sullen crowds lined the streets as the black soldiers came by, headed by a brass band and a giant coloured drum-major. The Germans resented this use of coloured troops as a deliberate humiliation to them. Stories of unpleasant incidents soon began to circulate. I was convinced it was a huge mistake on the part of France, even viewed from the standpoint of her own interests, and wrote to London urging the Society of Friends to use every possible influence to persuade the French Government to replace the coloured troops with whites.'

On both sides the skin was raw and nerves were touchy, yet fair-minded observers who got near to the real situation in Germany in 1920 were sure that the chance existed to 'win the peace' with a certainty that might have saved Europe from Hitler and a second catastrophic war.[1]

One day in Nuremberg J.T.B. saw huge processions of unarmed civilians in the streets, demonstrating against the Kapp *putsch*, an attempted counter-revolution by the old monarchist-nationalist gang: 'I believe it was during the Kapp *putsch* that the swastika was displayed for the first time as the symbol of a "new nationalism". The Republican Government fled from Berlin to Dresden but President Ebert advised the people to fight the *putsch* by a general strike. There was a total standstill of everything, railways and other transport, posts and telegraphs, public services, and most shops and schools. So effective was this passive resistance by the common people that on the fourth day the Kapp revolt collapsed. I have often wondered, in the light of subsequent

---
[1] See Vernon Bartlett's evidence in his book *This is my Life* (Chatto & Windus), 1938.

events, whether the Allies did not miss a golden opportunity, when the German people were in that mood, to have stepped in and given both moral and material support for two or three years until a real democratic and peace-pursuing Germany had become firmly established. Had that been so, subsequent history might have been very different.'

One thing that appalled J.T.B. was the difference between the Germany he saw and the picture painted in some sections of the Press: 'We had many opportunities of visiting German homes and institutions, and of studying the attitudes of mind of the people, and as our work continued we realized how widely our impressions differed from the statements which were appearing at the time in some (not all) British newspapers concerning famine conditions, which they alleged were much exaggerated, and concerning the state of mind of the German people. I think the correspondents of such newspapers relied too much for their information on the occupants of the luxury hotels where they stayed, and where black-market practices were common. I found that the decent-minded German was too proud to parade his misery to such journalists.'

Among J.T.B.'s papers are some notes that he used when addressing meetings in Germany. They show the line *he* took:

1. The world is dissatisfied with the old ways of life.
2. Force is no remedy; it does not necessarily prove which side is right; only which is stronger.
3. Militarism brings death, sorrow, despair, famine, misery, debt. It may remove some evils but it creates a host of others.
4. The world needs more than ever a way of life according to Christ's teaching and example.
5. Christianity is the whole of life, not a mere profession nor a division of life.
6. Service to others, not their domination, should be our purpose.

Mission of Peace

7. Love—not power, or fear, or jealousy.
8. The good of one individual or nation makes for the good of all.
9. The suffering of one individual or nation makes for the suffering of all.

His comment after speaking throughout Germany on these lines was: 'Many Germans were out of sympathy with professional religion. I found an increasing scorn for those who preached war. And I, an Englishman, had never an ill or angry word spoken to me at any meeting or elsewhere.'

Yet when the Quakers first applied to the British authorities after the war, for leave to go into Germany, one of the officials said: 'You had better take arms if you go to those places.'

One Sunday afternoon during the Kapp *putsch*, when the streets of Munich were heavily guarded and patrolled by republican soldiers (and somewhere in its beer cellars an unknown Hitler was fathering the Nazi movement), J.T.B. had an appointment with Pastor Burgmayr, head of the Baptist community of the city, who had been imprisoned at Knockaloe. At a tramway stop they met and were walking along the road when a formidably armed and steel-helmeted soldier came towards them. He looked suspiciously at the red-and-black star on J.T.B.'s armband, stopped him, and demanded to know what it represented.

'Pastor Burgmayr introduced me as a Quaker, and told of our work. I was watching the soldier's face and noticed his sternness relax. Then he said: "We have to be extra careful at times like this." I happened to have on me some leaflets about the Quaker relief work, printed in German, so I offered one to the trooper. As he took it he read its title, then looked at me quizzically and made a gesture at his rifle and bayonet, the bandolier of cartridges across his chest and the grenades slung from his belt. Then I noticed that the title of the leaflet I had given him was Der Waffen der Liebe (The Weapons of Love).

'The soldier smiled, folded the leaflet and put it in his belt wallet, clicked his heels, saluted, and went on his way.'

Craftsman and Quaker

Back in London, J.T.B. and Joan Fry, another of the Quaker workers in Germany, were asked to call at the Foreign Office to give a confidential report. Then J.T.B. wrote a detailed statement on his journey. It included this sentence:

'Give ye them to eat,' I seemed to hear the Master saying: if this is not heeded I fear there will arise so blinded a fury of desperate revolt that it may engulf not Germany alone but her neighbours also.

AND NEXT:

War in Ireland, the scene of J.T.B.'s next mission in 1921

Cartoon by Low from The Star

X

When Irish Eyes Aren't Smiling

It had been an unexpected and yet a consistent journey from his father's carpentry shop at Sheffield to the confidential interview at the Foreign Office; now J.T.B. must get back to teaching. He had used up all his savings and must return to 'normal'.

The old dream of working in a school with an enlightened art and craft policy was still with him; his experience of crafts and his capacity for handling people had been immensely broadened by his work during the war. He took a job at Cheltenham, to establish the handicrafts department in a new central school. If it wasn't the school of his dreams, it was a re-start along 'normal' lines.

He soon found that he was not destined to escape the abnormality of post-war life. In 1921 an urgent message from the Friends' Relief Committee sent him packing, during his school holidays, to an Ireland torn by civil war.

It would hardly be true to say that the Irish Republican Government and its Sinn Fein army, the IRA, were 'underground' organizations; they were illegal in the eyes of English and Ulstermen, but they were virtually in control of large areas of southern Ireland. Throughout the country and in the streets of Dublin itself there was bitter fighting. It was especially ruthless between the IRA and the Black-and-Tans, a force of British armed police recruited to suppress the rebels. Thousands of young Irishmen were rounded up in motor-lorries and taken to internment camps, under suspicion of disloyalty to the British Crown. 'When I landed at Kingstown (now called Dun Laoghaire) armed cars were guarding the quay, and as each passenger came ashore he was closely scrutinised by detectives and Black-and-Tans. The

Craftsman and Quaker

streets of Dublin were patrolled by lorries packed with tin-helmeted soldiers holding their rifles and revolvers at the ready. The ruins of the General Post Office and the bullet-pocked marks on walls and pavements were evidence of the Easter Rebellion of 1916 and the struggle which had gone on ever since. I was met by Samuel Graveson, representing the Friends' Relief Committee. We went to a Dublin hotel, and had no sooner entered the vestibule than there was a loud bang, the clatter of broken glass and a fusillade of shots. From the hotel lounge ran a woman with blood streaming from a cut face.

' "They're giving you a warm welcome, James," said Samuel Graveson.

'When I looked into the street a few minutes later there was every appearance of normality; ambushes had become a common feature of Dublin life. On this occasion, we were told, a bomb had been thrown at a passing motor-car containing British officers coming from a cricket match. The British returned fire, but no one was badly hurt, only the hotel was damaged.'

Samuel Graveson and James T. Baily visited two internment camps. It was a familiar scene to J.T.B., with the old problem of morale. The two Quakers attended at Dublin Castle for a conference with General Sir Neville Macready, the Commander of the British Forces in Ireland. On the way there Samuel Graveson remarked that on a previous occasion when he had met Sir Neville they had discussed reconciliation and the general had exclaimed: 'Would you have me go cap in hand to the Sinn Feiners?'

'Why go cap in hand?' Samuel Graveson had replied. 'Why not with one hand out-stretched for peace and reconciliation?'

Now Sir Neville greeted them warmly and called in his adjutant and his secretary. J.T.B. told of his work at Knockaloe, reported on what he had seen in the Irish internment camps, and suggested similar methods of occupational therapy.

'I think this is excellent,' said the general. 'If you people wish to go ahead on these lines I can promise all facilities in the camps.'

Irish Quakers acted on J.T.B.'s recommendations, and thus a

When Irish Eyes Aren't Smiling

new chapter of reconciliation began, but happily any large organization proved not to be needed as peace came soon afterwards between the English and the Irish, with the signing of the treaty that established the Irish Free State.

It is not generally known that during the last years of the Anglo-Irish troubles, when the smiling land of Ireland was bathed in tears and blood, and when the leaders on either side were only on shooting terms, one of the few secret avenues left open for getting them back on speaking terms was through the Quakers. One evening in a Dublin house J.T.B. had a long conversation with Edith Ellis, an English Quaker who was secretly travelling 'between the lines'; such people had the confidence of both sides. 'I marvelled at the courage of this remarkable woman,' says J.T.B.'s diary. (Edith Ellis was the daughter of John Edward Ellis, MP, Under-Secretary for India in the 1906 Liberal Government: her twin sister Marion became the second wife of Lord Parmoor, father of Sir Stafford Cripps.)

When antipathies become so bitter as to make direct contact impossible, such go-between activities are so delicate that little or nothing can be made public about them. They are not reported in the Press. But they have long been part of the Quaker work for international understanding, from the occasion when Joseph Sturge personally interviewed the Czar of Russia at the time of the Crimean War, to recent contact with the Communists of the Kremlin.

Some prophetic sentences were written by J.T.B. after his return from Ireland:

'With more knowledge of Ireland and of Irishmen will come a change in the attitude of most of us, and we shall, unless blinded by a false patriotism, be prepared ourselves to grant that for which Englishmen so stoutly asserted that they went to war with Germany—the rights of small nations. Greater knowledge is often what is needed as a first step towards the lessening of international and racial mistrusts and hatreds.'

Not long after his return J.T.B. was asked to give a lecture on the Friends' relief services at Ackworth, a large Quaker boarding

Craftsman and Quaker

school in Yorkshire. The headmaster, Gerald K. Hibbert, M.A., B.D., showed him over the school. Woodwork, said Mr Hibbert, was taken as an out-of-school hobby by the boys, under the guidance of the village carpenter. There were no crafts lessons at Ackworth.

'The subject has never been on the curriculum,' said the headmaster.

J.T.B. was shocked and said so. He peeped through a broken window into an adjoining building.

'That's the old gymnasium,' said the head. 'It's little used now, except for storing bicycles and junk.'

'It would make quite a useful metalwork shop,' his visitor remarked. He little thought how soon he would be turning it into a metalwork shop.

Over coffee that evening the craftsman talked with all his enthusiasm of crafts, and of the teaching of them, and the headmaster listened and, no doubt, weighed up this enthusiast who was saying things which might have sounded heretical to a public-school head less far-seeing than Gerald Hibbert.

A few weeks later J.T.B. travelled again to Yorkshire, this time to be interviewed for the job of full-time crafts master at Ackworth.

'I jumped at what seemed to be the chance of a lifetime, the opportunity to build on virgin ground. Ackworth was a school of the old-established grammar school type, and here was the chance to bring craftwork into balance with the academic subjects, which is I believe the right equilibrium. Further, Ackworth was a boarding school, something new to me. And, best of all, it was a Quaker school. All the experiences of my life now seemed to be drawing together and bringing me to this opportunity.'

XI

Mr Chips Finds His Home

One of the villagers of Ackworth was once invited to subscribe to a fund for the building of a wall round the churchyard. He replied:

'Naay, what's t'use of a wall? Them what's inside can't get out, an' them what's outside doesn't want ti be in.'

The story is typical of the dourness, the common-sense, and the humour of the people of this part of England. These were qualities that J.T.B. knew very well; he had returned to Yorkshire, to a part not many miles from his boyhood home at Sheffield. The countryside of the West Riding of Yorkshire, like its people, is somewhat austere. The pastures and fields of corn have a habit of terminating abruptly in ugly pit-head dumps and colliery head-gear. Between Pontefract and Hemsworth stands the Quaker boarding school, solidly placed on high ground, built of grey stone weathered by the storms, with flagstones worn by the feet of generations of children.

Ackworth is the largest and one of the oldest and most renowned of the Quaker schools. It was founded in 1779 by a group of Quakers led by Dr John Fothergill, physician, philanthropist, and collaborator with John Howard in penal reform. It is now one of nine boarding schools run by the Society of Friends. The pupils are not necessarily Quakers—in fact, less than half of them come from Quaker families. But the schools are conducted in the Quaker tradition.

In this atmosphere J.T.B. settled down and lived and worked for fourteen years. He became the Mr Chips of Ackworth, and now that he has passed on they say he has become a legend in the school, a personality that will belong to it as long as memory and tradition endure.

Craftsman and Quaker

But it was not all easy going for Mr Chips. At his first interview he received this warning:

'It is only fair to tell you that I have decided to place crafts in the curriculum of the school despite the opposition of some of my staff, perhaps the majority. The man who is appointed to this job may not have a very comfortable time.

'The opposition,' the head explained, 'comes mainly from the older and more academic members of the staff. Rather naturally from their point of view, they may look upon you as an interloper in the curriculum. The time-table is already crowded, and they think that woodwork in a boy's spare time is all that is necessary. They don't think Ackworth is the sort of school where crafts need figure as a lesson subject.'

One morning soon after the new master had arrived he went at recess to the masters' common room where they were having their coffee, smoking and gossiping before resuming lessons. The room was full, and as J.T.B. went in he heard a voice protesting about 'this wretched subject, crafts'—taking up valuable time, said the complainant, some of which he sorely needed for his French lessons. Then the French master turned round, and said with a disarming smile: 'Sorry, J.T.B.—you're a good chap, but it's your wretched subject I object to.'

The only way was to press on cheerfully with the wretched subject; J.T.B. had the head's full support, and the school spent a large sum of money on alterations to premises and on new equipment. At last here was something like the crafts department of his dreams—not only a woodwork shop but a metalwork shop and forge, a spacious drawing-office, and a light crafts shop for book-binding, leather working, raffia work and basket making, rug-making, and light woodwork.

An even wider range would have pleased J.T.B. still more—pottery, for example—for he believed that during a boy's (or girl's) school life he should be given the opportunity to try his hand at a variety of handwork. Not all children have a natural aptitude for woodwork, but often a boy who is all thumbs with a chisel in his hands becomes an adept at a more plastic craft such as clay modelling (or vice versa). In the years after his retirement, pottery and other crafts were introduced at Ackworth by J.T.B.'s successors. So are good foundations built upon, to the greater good of those who follow.

To some extent the crafts at Ackworth were integrated with the art department of the school. All his life J.T.B. had preached that craftwork lessons should be related to other subjects such as mathematics, geography, and art. This did not go as far as J.T.B. had hoped.

'There were some things I did not get, but I felt that "step by step" was the best policy. Sometimes ideals cannot be achieved, and even have to be temporarily abandoned. This was so at Ackworth with regard to the problem of exams. When I went there the head and I agreed not to make crafts an examination subject, either for internal terminal examinations or for school certificate. We wanted the boys to enjoy the work for its own sake, not for exam placings. This ambition broke down. I found that boys were being kept back from craft lessons by certain masters, to give more time to academic subjects—"It won't matter to your exam results if you miss craft." I was compelled to ask the head to place the workshops on the same level vis-à-vis exams as the science labs and academic classrooms; this was expedient if they were to attain equal status and prestige in the eyes of staff, of students, and of parents and boys. It happened that at this very time the Northern Universities Examinations Board decided to include handicrafts and technical drawing in the School Certificate, so we henceforth entered boys for these subjects. They were so successful it was almost an embarrassment to me, because I would never allow the pursuit of exam results to become a fetish.

'Gradually the crafts department proved its worth at Ackworth. Into this old-established school the training of eye and hand came to be accepted as a natural part of education, as natural as a training in English or mathematics or Latin. This, I strongly believe, had a healthy effect on school life; it also benefited particular boys who might otherwise have fallen by the

Craftsman and Quaker

roadside. It is a fallacy that only the "dull" boys need craftwork, or that only the "non-academic types" make good craftsmen; some of the best boys and girls I have ever known at woodwork and metalwork were also the "brainy" ones. But they benefited by the more all-round education that crafts gave them.

'And as for the so-called "dull" boy, of course he finds a new world when he discovers an ability in craft. There was the case of J.A., a boy who came to Ackworth from Newcastle-on-Tyne. Book-work was an awful grind for him, but in the workshops he was transformed. To set the bellows blowing until a bright red flaming cone of fire blazed in the forge, and to draw from it a piece of iron glowing and sparkling, to swing it quickly on to the anvil and bring the hammer to work with ringing blows—this was a joyous satisfaction to the boy. Or one would find J.A. happily crouched over the lathe; it became the custom when a master wanted J.A. in out-of-lesson hours to direct another boy to fetch him from the metal-work shop! He became one of my most apt pupils, tools were natural to him, and his resourceful and inventive capacity was remarkable. He read the technical magazines and books which were placed in the workshop library, and had no difficulty in working out mathematical calculations necessary for any practical work he had in hand. But unfortunately in the opinion of some of my colleagues he was unworthy of the school because he did not show interest and success in the more academic subjects.

'One day the head called me into his study and told me that members of the staff were urging that J.A.'s guardian be asked to transfer him to a technical school. What did I think?

' "This boy," I replied, "is an outstanding success at the crafts. He is excellent at mechanical drawing. He is interested in any parts of science or other subjects which he sees to have any relationship to craftsmanship. Quite apart from these abilities, I think he is receiving at Ackworth a good grounding in many things suited to his natural development, and this will stand him in good stead when he undertakes some technical education, which he should have *not now* but later on. To send him away would be bad for him psychologically. Here at Ackworth he realizes he lags behind his contemporaries in academic scholarship, but this is cancelled out when he sees himself far outstripping them in practical and creative attainments, and thus his self-respect and confidence are maintained."

'The head agreed. J.A. stayed on. When his School Certificate year came round, the head took an unusual action. He asked the University Examinations Board to allow J.A. to sit for the woodwork, metalwork, and technical drawing papers only, for he was almost sure to fail at other subjects. Should he satisfy the examiners in these subjects, the head asked them to issue a special letter to that effect. The board agreed. J.A. passed highly in his subjects, and got his letter. I was delighted by this breaking with the examination fetish and putting the boy first, and it enhanced my admiration of a great and liberal-minded headmaster.

'The sequel came in the 1940s when during a visit to Newcastle-on-Tyne I met J.A. I visited the optical and scientific instrument-making business he was running at Gateshead. He had designed and manufactured some original and very successful photographic apparatus, and was making high-precision machinery for turbine research, and special apparatus for medical research, all of which he showed me with great pride.'

It was a remarkable revolution that Gerald K. Hibbert, a scholar and theologian, had instigated at Ackworth. He himself said about it:

'I feel more and more the value of good craftsmanship, possibly because I was never a good craftsman myself. I feel the loss, and keenly regret the blank in my life. No boy or girl should go out from Ackworth without an opportunity of being a good craftsman. A boy or girl who becomes a good craftsman at sixteen is on the way to become a good citizen. I am of opinion that every school of this sort should have effective workshops established in connection with it.'[1]

[1] Quoted from the Annual Report of the Ackworth School Old Scholars' Association, 1924.

Craftsman and Quaker

Every revolution has its pangs, then the new becomes the normal. As the years passed Mr Chips of Ackworth grew into the fabric of the school, finding in its varied life a full satisfaction for his enthusiasms. He lived in a house nearby; the tinkling of the bell floated down amid the distant shouts and whistles of boys to warn him of the time for lessons or duties. He took his turn as master-on-duty, superintending the boys in out-of-lessons hours, taking them to the swimming bath or games field, giving permissions for this and that, and keeping a weather eye open for the scrimshankers and mischief-makers: 'One learns to turn a blind eye to some escapades, and to deal sufficiently severely with over-boisterous practical-jokers and the occasional bullies. Usually in a school where the staff are on terms of friendship and respect with the boys the natural exuberance of youth can be sublimated to harmless ends. The games side of the school is important in this respect. At Ackworth the crafts department came to fulfil a similar purpose. Out-of-school hours found many boys voluntarily working off their energies there. The sartorially minded began a craze for making trouser-presses, for which I bought the metal fittings in large quantities. To have one's legs encased in trousers showing a knife-edge became a mark of culture, and to be able to make an efficient press was a step far in advance of the traditional Ackworth method of placing one's "bags" between mattress and bedclothes.

'Long before winter came, far-seeing boys spent many hours in the workshop making sledges. All sizes and designs were produced, the woodwork was brightly painted, and the iron runners were wrought in the forge, and well-shaped and fixed. When snow came the sledges were proudly brought out and pulled to Primrose Vale for the exhilarating sport there to be had.

'Sunday afternoon duty involved, during my earlier years at Ackworth, taking the lower forms on a long walk known as a pig drive. This communal hike was unpopular, and later when a change of headmaster from Gerald Hibbert to Arthur Cooper brought its abolition, the jubilation of the boys was expressed by the construction of an image of a large pig, with fireworks

Mr Chips Finds His Home

attached to it. On November 5th this effigy was solemnly paraded to the chanting of topical doggerels, and then hurled into the flames of a bonfire. It had become one of my unofficial duties to superintend the building of the bonfire each year for Guy Fawkes' Day, so on this occasion I had to assume the role of chief priest at the obsequies of the pig drive.

'Some of the Ackworth doggerels are of unknown age, having been passed down from generation to generation of scholars. As the term drew to its end youthful voices would be heard chanting these lines, and variations thereof which poetic inspiration contrived from year to year:

> No more Latin, no more French,
> No more swotting on top bench.
>
> No more spiders in my bath,
> Trying hard to make me laugh.
>
> No more stew and semolina,
> No more meat that could be leaner.
>
> No more tadpoles in my tea,
> Making googly eyes at me.
>
> No more pillows stuffed with sticks,
> No more mattresses made of bricks.'

During his fourteen years at Ackworth J.T.B. rode the flood tide of his life. His sense of humour, his practical skills, his interest in human beings *as* human beings and not as mere specimens in a schoolmaster's case-book, all came into full play; and the quality which above all others earned him the respect of his boys and girls was his combination of practicality with idealism. This characteristic was not only the natural development of his own history and personality: it was his reaction to the attitude of the people called Quakers. Quakerism appealed to him as the application of Christian values to daily living, in wartime and in peace; and in a Quaker school his own qualities grew strong in such an atmosphere.

Craftsman and Quaker

Idealism appeals to youth, which has (or should have) no room for the crabbed cynicism of the aged and disillusioned, but which can equally well detect that false high-mindedness which is made of pious platitudes and windy aspirations. In their Mr Chips the boys of Ackworth found a man who had kept his ideals fresh (there was never anything of the cynic about him) and yet had his feet planted firmly on the ground. Who can say what character-building influence this had? Hundreds of boys came his way, to pass in due time into a wider world; hundreds of names and faces he remembered, and many came back in later years to look him up. After he had retired and was living at Welwyn Garden City a knock sometimes came at the door and on the threshold stood a matured man, perhaps a city gent in bowler and rolled umbrella, or a bearded architect, or a soldier in uniform—'Don't you remember me, sir?'—and J.T.B. would look twice and think back over all those hundreds of boys . . . now, which one was this?

There was Glen Glasier, son of John Bruce Glasier, a sturdy Socialist who had come out of Scotland at the turn of the century to join William Morris, Bernard Shaw, Keir Hardie and the other pioneers in founding the Labour Party. To find Bruce Glasier's son in his care at Ackworth took J.T.B. back to the days of his own early political enthusiasms. Glen's mother, Katharine Bruce Glasier, became one of J.T.B.'s closest friends through her visits to her son while he was at Ackworth. As Katharine St John Conway she had been another of the great-hearted pioneers of the British Labour movement. The son, Glen, had inherited high intellectual qualities and a ready wit. Once, when on holiday from Ackworth, he had an encounter with H. G. Wells at an ILP summer school in Essex. The schoolboy, aged fourteen, was sitting next to the author and sociologist, who later described how he had 'happened to say, a bit carelessly perhaps, that the Japanese could not colonise'.

'What right have you to say that?' asked Glen Glasier.

'What right have you to challenge it?' replied the author of *The Outline of History*.

Mr Chips Finds His Home

'It depends what you mean by colonise,' said Glen. 'If you mean that the Japanese can't hold a country down imperialist fashion, and govern it, look at their work in Korea. If you mean that they can't go into another country and settle there and farm successfully, ask the Australians why they are so afraid to let them come in: and look what they have done all round San Francisco.'

Telling this story later, H. G. Wells remarked: 'I took off my hat to the boy. He has his father's spirit.'

Glen Glasier's short life was linked in a remarkable way with J.T.B.'s long life. In 1927 Glen won an open scholarship from Ackworth to Oxford, but first he went temporarily as a student master to the Friends' School, Saffron Walden, in Essex. He was playing football there with the boys one March afternoon; Laurence Housman was watching from the touch-line and (he writes): 'I saw the boy fall, and as he lay so still with never a movement I began to have a dread of what might have happened.' Glen, aged eighteen, was dead. He lies now in the quiet Quaker burial ground at Saffron Walden. After his death some of his letters were published; through them rings not only the spirit of his parents but the influence of his craftsmaster at Ackworth:

'I believe like you that England is over-industrialized, and the lack of creative toil close to nature is responsible for many of the blights of our machine civilization.'

How that must have cheered J.T.B.'s heart after the loss of such a pupil. And this, written by Glen to his sister in Australia: 'I am convinced that until we get rid of the appalling ignorance of the masses and educate them to use their power and leisure rightly, at home, at the workshop, and at the ballot box, we are running a terrible risk and imperilling the whole of civilization.'

And: 'This is not a stupid Utopianism; the world may yet permit the craftsman's joy to exist once more. All my father's and William Morris's work showed us the way.'

J.T.B.'s comment on this was: 'The idealism of youth, which shone through young Glen Glasier, as it has shone through so many of my old boys, is not to be scoffed at. It is our Yesterday asking us what we have lost of the old brave spirit.'

Craftsman and Quaker

In that last sentence the tragedy as well as the triumph of J.T.B.'s life is revealed. It is the tragedy and triumph of all sensitive people who have lived through the past half century: tragedy that the lion-hearted idealism of their youth should have been rewarded with two devastating wars and a modern world where the H-bomb invokes a shrug of the shoulders, and in which the materialist pessimism of the masses is expressed in that fatuously lily-hearted phrase 'I couldn't care less'; triumph, in that the things of the spirit work in mysterious ways, so that the flash of a phrase from a Glen Glasier may illuminate the darkness with an assurance that the power of the good and courageous is not dead.

History is full of victories of the spirit snatched out of apparent defeat. Dark seemed the fate of Beethoven, dogged by illness and misfortune, yet his spirit rose indomitably to the heights and left to the world a revelation of the sublime in his music, the more victorious because some of the greatest of it was written when he was stone deaf. Dark was the lot of the early Quakers, George Fox and his contemporaries, in the days of their religious persecution; when they lay in the black and stinking holes of English dungeons there must have seemed in moments of despair to be no hope for the things they believed in. There have been many Calvaries since the supreme one. Bestial was Belsen, and Buchenwald was horror unthinkable, yet the world has since been uplifted by the stories of many valiant spirits who snatched victory from that defeat—as in the case of Sophie Scholl, a girl of twenty-one, who wrote before they killed her:

After all, one should have the courage to believe in what is good. I do not mean that one should believe in illusions, but I mean that one should do only what is true and good and take it for granted that other people will do the same, in a way one can never do with the intellect alone. That is to say—*never calculate.*

The courage to believe in what is good is not an easy virtue. James Thomas Baily, who whilst an optimist and a humanitarian, was also very sensitive to the changing moods of the world, had

Mr Chips Finds His Home

to fight the temptation to become embittered and disillusioned when the enthusiasm and idealism of his young manhood were rewarded with the evils of the First World War; and when between the wars he saw, at close quarters, Europe throwing away all hope of winning the peace; and when a Second World War brought, seemingly, the bankruptcy of Christian pity and human dignity in saturation bombing and Hiroshima and the ultimate blasphemy of the H-bomb. This was too much to accept with equanimity; most people looked the other way—'Such things don't bear thinking about'. J.T.B. at eighty looked evil in the face as boldly as at eighteen. He remained to the end an optimist for the things of the spirit, a humanitarian in an increasingly de-humanised world, but at times the cup was bitter for the schoolmaster who saw, with some resentment, two generations of his boys fed to the cannon. One day during his retirement he went back to St Albans:

'I stood before the war memorial in St Peter's Street, and as my eye ran down the long list of names I counted over eighty of those whom I had taught at the handicrafts centre there between 1897 and 1911. As my eye read each name there passed before my inner vision a face, young and eager.

'Arthur Wiggs—a humble working-class lad who did so well at crafts that I took him when he came to school-leaving age as a pupil teacher . . . as I read his name I felt that the blithe spirit who had taken the torch from me in the relay race had been tripped up and robbed of his chance.

'Hilliard . . . Pellant . . . Hiskett . . . Peters . . . Massey . . . Hunt. . . . I read down the lists until my eyes filled with tears. I saw again the boyish hands, handling saw and plane, clumsily at first, then with efficiency and joy as increasing skill poured through their fingers. How evil a fate that turned those hands to destructive ends.'

Would there never be an end to man's inhumanity? When the newspapers told of the persecution of the Jews and their exodus from the Nazi lands an elderly retired teacher who had 'done his whack' might have been excused for washing his hands of it all and sitting back to vegetate in his remaining years; but not J.T.B. In the late 1930s, when refugees from Germany and Austria were pouring into England, the Friends' Peace Committee asked him to take charge of a reception centre which, in its peculiar Quakerish method, was much more than a reception centre. It was in its way a miracle. A burnt-out mansion on the bank of a beautiful creek off the River Fal in Cornwall was offered to the Society of Friends; one wing could be made habitable by hard work, and J.T.B. was given charge of turning it into a training-cum-holiday centre for refugees, where (and here is the special Quaker touch) Jew and Gentile would live and work together. As the warden of Carclew House he had the job of deploying a very mixed labour force to put the place in order, and of being their host and adviser in a strange land:

'Our idea was that Carclew should be a place where they could spend some weeks or months, finding a home, doing useful work, enjoying the Cornish coast, assimilating themselves to English life after their terrible experiences in Europe, and living in comradeship with people of differing nationalities and faiths. In running the place English Quakers had the help of the IVSP (International Voluntary Service for Peace), an organization which had originated in Switzerland and in which young men and women of all nationalities combined to carry out much valuable relief work. We had at times as many as fifty people at Carclew—refugees, Quaker workers, and IVSP personnel. There was very hard manual labour to do, but we tried to balance it with good companionship at meals, with concerts, sing-songs, discussions, walks and excursions to various parts of Cornwall, and there was a short meeting for worship every morning.'

It was not an easy team for J.T.B. to run. Many of the refugees arrived resentful, harmed bodily and mentally by their abuse at the hands of the Nazis. The voluntary workers were themselves an odd assortment—an Egyptian university student who gave up his vacation to do work of this kind, a couple of sturdy Swedes and a young woman from the same country who so captivated one of the English helpers that she became his wife, a head gardener who was 'a Swiss of uncertain temperament, but he knew how to cultivate the Carclew wilderness and turn it into a garden'.

Carclew was a typical Quaker experiment in reconciliation. It made its mistakes and had its failures, but the essence of the purpose may be seen in the story of Alfred the Viennese. It is a story which, in a sense, sums up the life of J.T.B. for it shows at one and the same time the two avenues through which he followed the widening quest: his search for Christian understanding and his belief in the healing power of craftsmanship.

'When Alfred first arrived we were busy in the fire-blackened ruins of Carclew laying new floors, fitting doors, painting and cleaning, making drains, and putting the gardens in order. He was a little dark man, very subdued, with a look of tragic suffering on his face. I showed him round. Some of the dilapidated rooms had been restored and fitted as dormitories with rows of double-decker wooden bedsteads, but were otherwise unfurnished. Alfred was very silent during the tour, and I noticed a look of grim disappointment on his face. Then the storm burst. In a torrent of angry protests he said he had not known what sort of place he was coming to, he wished to be near London so that he could easily go to Dover when his wife and child came from Vienna, now he found himself three hundred miles away, etc., etc. His voice broke, and then, mastering his sobs, he said: "But, sir!—you are now my master, you will give me my orders and I shall obey."

'Taking Alfred by the arm, I led him across the lawn and endeavoured to sooth his frayed nerves, explaining that Carclew was not a place of master and servants, of orders and obedience, but a community striving to work together for the common good. "We are friends and equals," I said.

'It was fully two months later that I came to know the reason of his being a refugee (it was wise to restrain one's curiosity in all such cases). One Sunday morning as the two of us walked to Falmouth Friends' Meeting House, Alfred told me he had been a scenic artist and property man in one of the Vienna theatres;

Craftsman and Quaker

he was a supporter of the Hapsburg monarchy and a member of a secret party plotting the restoration of the royal house. When the Nazis came to power in Austria, Alfred tried to destroy papers which would incriminate his colleagues. He was taken to prison and tortured to make him divulge their names, but without that result. He was eventually released through the mediation of a friend who was "in with the police", and he escaped from Austria to England. He was haunted by fears for his wife and daughter until the Quaker centre in Vienna got into touch with them and news came through to Carclew that they would leave for England in August, 1939.

'During the period of waiting for their arrival Alfred took an interest in a top-floor room which had been completely blackened by soot during the fire, and its paintwork badly blistered. Alfred was continually making little sketch plans for its renovation, and one day he asked me if the top-floor room might be entrusted to him, and that it should be kept locked until his work in it was completed. He became a new man. His moroseness disappeared. He scraped and washed the soot away, burned off and renewed the paint, and decorated the walls and beams with brightly coloured designs representing the four seasons and portraying Austrian scenes. At last came the day when it was thrown open for all to see. What surprise and congratulations!

'Not long after this the Cornish Riviera express steamed into Truro station, and a small flaxen-haired girl appeared at a window calling "Papa! Papa!" Alfred, on the platform, replied "Lotta! Lotta!" He bounded along to embrace his daughter. Behind the little girl came a fair young woman whose eyes were brimming with tears of joy. Alfred and his family were reunited. Their suitcases contained all that remained of their possessions. As soon as they reached Carclew Alfred took them to see the top-floor room, and what a rejoicing there was when they saw its Viennese decoration. A few hours later I called upon them.

' "Well, Alfred, settling in all right?" I asked.

' "Yes, Father B," he replied (he always called me Father B). "But just look"—he took his wife's head between his hands—

16

The Carclew experiment 1939: the Mansion in Cornwall, and the Warden (J. T. B.) in his 'Office'

J. T. B. with the younger generation; he lectures on his Quaker Relief work in the First World War to trainees at the Hampstead hostel of the Friends Relief Service, 1940

Mr Chips Finds His Home

"see those grey hairs?—all have come since I left Vienna ten months ago."

' "I see them," I said. "But you must not heed them now. Happier days are before you."

'This proved to be true. Alfred's wife lost her wan look. Alfred was completely restored to health of body and mind. Later, he set up in business as a tailor in an English town, where he has prospered.'

When war came again the Friends' Relief Service was expanded until it employed some 1,200 people at home and abroad. Again Father B's experience was requisitioned, this time as a combined clerk-of-works and humanitarian-in-charge at a mansion at Flax Bourton, near Bristol, which was converted into a 'sick bay' for evacuee children who came from the slums and were so dirty and infested with fleas and lice that it was impossible to send them into ordinary homes. Medical men and psychologists were co-opted to Flax Bourton, and an experienced nursing sister was appointed matron. Volunteers came as nurses, domestic helpers, and handy-men: 'They did a grand piece of work, often of a repulsive nature. I remember a batch of fresh arrivals having to be de-loused, their clothing destroyed, and their hair shorn. The nurse called me in to look at the water in the bath after this operation. It had a floating scum of dead lice. Clothing, feeding and cleansing the children was not enough, of course. We started educational work. We gave them lessons in craft work with paper, pencils, crayons, and paints, and simple woodwork.'

To the smallest and humblest and most needy he gave with both hands, he whose own life had begun in a humble carpenter's shop at Sheffield.

During three score years and ten he passed his skill and enthusiasms to thousands of people, to evacuees and refugees, to prisoners of war and Borstal boys, to adults and schoolboys, and to his own children and grandchildren who came to the little workshop behind the house of his retirement at Welwyn Garden City, to watch him working at his bench amid 'the sweet smell of sawdust', just as he as a boy had watched his father.

Craftsman and Quaker

'As I work at my bench, memories of my boyhood are repeatedly revived by the sight of the silent witnesses about me: the tools my father used so competently, and which I use now. I remember how he treated them with such care and consideration, as though they were living helpmates. There before me as I work are his three rows of planes, his chisels, his saws. Often, while holding in my hands one of the tools my father held in his, my fingers and thumbs gripping and guiding where his did, my palms pressing where his palms pressed, my eyes and mind intent on attaining the desired end as his eyes and mind were, I have wondered whether some subtle influence was mysteriously transferred to me through that tool. I know that throughout life I have caught some of the same creative joy which was manifest in my father's life.

'The other day one of my grandchildren came to my workshop and said to me, "Grandad, show me how to make the joints of this cupboard." I showed him, and then he set to work on the joints, using my tools—his great-grandfather's tools—and it was a joy to me to see the dexterity of his fingers. One of my greatest rewards was when my granddaughter, while still a schoolgirl at Ackworth, brought home a really beautiful bookrack she had made, and a stool in oak. In her last year at school she was permitted to select her lesson subjects, and she chose woodwork for one; she was, I believe, the first girl in the long history of Ackworth school to take lessons in the school workshops.'

The right place of crafts in a general education continued to be his passionate interest long after his official retirement from teaching. It received a new impetus during the war when the headmaster of the Welwyn Garden City Grammar School, short of staff, asked him to go back to the classroom as part-time crafts teacher. Mr Nichol baited his hook with this sentence: 'You can try out all the "might-have-beens" in theory where you left off at Ackworth.'

So, for three wartime years J.T.B. was Mr Chips again: 'To some extent I was able to try out some of those pet ideas of mine, and I greatly enjoyed the work, but of course the fact is that a

Mr Chips Finds His Home

balanced education in England is, with a few rare and splendid exceptions, one of the "might-have-beens". The day when the crafts will rank equal in prestige with the academic subjects is yet to come. This, in an age when industralialism has virtually supplanted craftsmanship, is a catastrophe. Mass production of industrial articles, of motor-cars and clothing, of houses and furniture and pots and pans—all this is presumably necessary in our civilization, but it brings with it the worshipping of speed and utilitarianism and the machine, and a tendency to scorn the old-fashioned virtue of craftsmanship. The solution to this problem lies in the education of boys and girls. As machine production leads more and more to shorter hours, the right use of leisure assumes paramount importance for our happiness.

'In 1929 when a Fellowship of the College of Handicraft was conferred upon me, the Members of the College who were being raised to Fellows were charged by the President in these words:

' "The age in which we are living is not conducive to a development of hand skill in creative work. The love for beautiful, handmade craft work can only, to any appreciable extent, be cultivated in the schools, and it is here that you, as teachers and craftsmen and craftswomen, can do mighty work. Upon you rests the responsibility for keeping alive and fostering the traditions of fine craftsmanship which have been handed down to us through the ages." '

At eighty years of age James Thomas Baily died in The Retreat, the mental hospital at York, where the Society of Friends has for many years played a pioneer part in the modern treatment of psychic illness. A heart weakness had affected his brain, but even in this illness Mr Chips ran true to form: making a partial recovery so that he could leave the wards and walk or work as he willed about the hospital, J.T.B. made a bee-line for The Retreat's workshop. He was back at the bench, with chisel and plane, the loves of his life. This was his own occupational therapy, and for several months before the final relapse he found health in making bookracks and trays which he gave to the hospital and his friends. The cares of the outside world were

Craftsman and Quaker

forgotten in these last months of joyous craftsmanship. Then the quest was ended—or had it only just begun?

In those he had influenced, by example and by word, it most certainly continues.

The chain reaction in atomic physics is something we regard with wonder tinged by fear; the chain reactions of human behaviour and example can also work for good or for evil, and no one can tell their ultimate effect. The years pass by, then some incident occurs to remind us that a man's influence is not ended with his life. In 1947 when thousands of Nazis were held in concentration camps in Germany, a visitor from the Friends' Relief Service was astonished to find in one camp a group of Nazis (or ex-Nazis) studying Quakerism, of all things. He asked how this began and the leader of the group said he had been interned in Knockaloe during the First World War, and there had made his first contact with Quakers. Between the wars, he admitted, he had been mesmerised by the Hitler philosophy, but now he understood its falseness, and he and his friends were searching for a new and better faith.

In 1956 when Hungary was torn by revolt the Friends sent medical supplies into the country; one of their motor-lorries was damaged in an accident in a remote district, but its crew got help from a garage. Inspecting the wreckage, the Hungarian garage proprietor saw the red-and-black star painted on the side.

'You are belonging to the Friends—the Quakers?' he asked excitedly. 'In the First World War I knew a Quaker. I was then a prisoner in the Isle of Man. He gave me tools, and something to do. He was a good man.'

The damaged truck was repaired in the Hungarian garage—so well that it came back to England a better vehicle than it went out.

In 1957 James Thomas Baily was buried in the grounds of the Quaker Meeting House at Sibford on the edge of the Cotswolds. His sons, seeking some lines to print on the card advising J.T.B.'s wide circle of friends that he had passed on, turned to his *Crafts Anthology*: the book, published in 1953, in which he

Mr Chips Finds His Home

had printed a life-time's collection of quotations taken from his wide reading on crafts and craftsmanship. They found these lines from a poem called *The City* by the modern Quaker poet William R. Hughes:

> See where the craftsman's last touch lingers
> To draw the wonder from the wood,
> As life and love, poured through his fingers,
> Create and call it good.

A few days later a letter came from William R. Hughes: 'Did you know that when I wrote those lines I had your father in mind?'

They did not know, but they were not surprised that once again was shown the mystic influence of a dedicated life.

INDEX

Ackworth School, 121 et seq.
Adult Schools, 70, 80
Albany, USA, 76
Allott, Lucy, 50, 53, 60, 64
Allott, Percy, 64
America, United States of, 74 et seq.
Angling, 28
Artisans' dress, 16
Ashford, Kent, 86

Baily, Alfred, 49
Baily, Annie (née Winter), 24
Baily, Fred, 29
Baily, Grandfather James (father of J.T.B.), 9, 10, 11, 12, 24, 37, 39, 46
Baily, Joseph William, 39, 40
Baily, Lucy—*see* Allott
Baily, Mary, 12, 13
Baily, Susannah, 11, 12, 23, 24, 46
Barbed-wire disease, 93
Basket-making in POW camp, 104
Bassett-Lowke, W. J., 102
Bennett, Prof. C. A., 40
Beveridge, William, 66
Board School in 1881, 18 et seq.
Boarding-school life, 123 et seq.
Boer War, 62, 68
Borstal Institution, 79 et seq.
Bottesford, Notts, 29
Bottomley, Horatio, 96

Cadbury, George, 65
Canada, 75 et seq.
Carclew, 134
Carpentry and joinery, 17, 43
'Catch-'em-Alive Man', 14
Celtic (liner) torpedoed, 103
Central School, 40, 55, 56
Chalmers, James, 48
Chatham, 79
Cheltenham, 52, 119

Christmas customs, 15
Churchill, Winston, 65, 66
City Temple, 45
Clark, Robert, 88
College of Handicraft, 139
Congregational Church, 23, 48, 49, 58, 72
Consumption (TB), 23, 48, 49
Country life, 29 et seq., 57
Courage, 132
Coward, Sir Henry, 32
Craft guilds, 36, 38
Craft teaching, 40, 52, 55, 75, 76, 77, 78, 84, 122, 124, 138, 139
Craftsmanship, 10, 11, 22, 29, 37, 38, 39, 42, 51, 52, 61, 65, 102, 138, 139

Daily Mail, 59
Daily News, 65
Dale, Robert W., 80
Disease, 25, 34
Drunkenness, 30

Eden, Sir Timothy, 94
Education Act, 1870, 11, 18
Education, Board of, 77
Elberfeld, 112
Ellis, Edith, 121
Engraving, 36
Entertainments, in the 'eighties, 14, 15
Entertainments, Edwardian, 60, 82
Errand-boy's work, 24, 25
Escapes from POW camp, 102
Essen, 114
Evacuees, 137
Examinations, school, 78, 125

Fisk Jubilee Singers, 45
Flax Bourton, near Bristol, 137
Foreign Office, 118

Index

Fothergill, Dr John, 123
France, 110
Frankfurt-on-Main, 114, 115
Friends' Ambulance Unit, 87, 91
Friends' Emergency Committee, 88
Friends' Peace Committee, 134
Friends' Relief Service, 137, 140
Friends, Society of—*see* Quakers
Friends' War Victims Relief Committee, 87, 109, 119
Fry, Joan, 117

Games, 26, 27
German band, 15
Germany, 109, 111 et seq.
Gillingham, 79
Glasier, Glen, 130, 131
Grammar Schools, 78, 122, 138
Graveson, Samuel, 120
Grimthorpe, Lord, 61

Halle, 114
Handforth Camp, Manchester, 89, 92
Hanover, 111
Hardie, Keir, 36, 47, 67
Harrod, J. T., 84
Hems, Harry, 61
Hibbert, G. K., 122, 127
Horsnaill, Alfred, 82
Horsnaill, Headley, 80
Hyndman, H. M., 32, 35

Imperialism, 31, 33
Independent Labour Party, 47
Independent Schools, 84
Industrial work in camps, 88 et seq.
Industrialism, 33, 59, 66, 139
Inflation, 112
Integration, 56, 125
International Voluntary Service for Peace, 134
Internment camps, 88 et seq.
Ireland, 119
Irish Civil War, 119 et seq.

Jones, Montague, 78

Jones, Rev. J. D., 48
Jubilee, Queen's, 32

Kapp *putsch*, 115, 117
Kent Education Committee, 79, 91, 96
Knitting, in POW camp, 101
Knockaloe Camp, 91 et seq.

Labour Party, 66
Lansbury, George, 66
Leipzig, 113
Liberalism, 20, 33, 36, 51, 60, 66
Lighting, in street and home, 23
Lincoln, 42 et seq.
Lloyd George, 66, 114
London Missionary Society, 25, 48
Lynn, Alfred, 70, 71
Lynn, Elizabeth, 72

Macready, General Sir Neville, 120
Man, Isle of, 92, 95, 104, 109
Manual Training Teachers, National Association of, 41, 52
Matt, Charles, 102, 109
Michelangelo, 43
Militarism, 109, 116
Missionaries, 48, 90
Morris, William, 35, 51, 65, 131
Mosely, Alfred, 75, 77
Mosely Commission, 74 et seq.
Muffin Man, 25
Mummers' plays, 15
Munich, 117

New York, 74
Niagara, 77
Nonconformity, 20
Nuremberg, 113, 115

Oldershaw, Sam, 51, 52

Pacifism, 68, 70, 91, 95, 96, 108, 114, 116
Pageant, St Albans, 62
Panzera, Lieut.-Col., 97

Index

Parents' and Teachers' Association, 76
Parker, Dr Joseph, 45
Penn, William, 83
Philadelphia High School, 76
Plumer, General, 144
Poverty, 25, 33, 34, 50, 65
Puritanism, 29 et seq.

Quaker schools, 84, 123 et seq.
Quakers, 68, 70, 72, 79, 83, 94, 96, 117, 120, 129, 134
Quayle-Dickson, Major, 98, 104

Refugees from Nazism, 134
Relief work in Europe, 108, 110 et seq., 137
Religious education, 20
Retreat, The, 139
Riley, J., 74
Ripper, Prof. W., 40
Rochester, 79, 80, 81
Rotten, Dr Elizabeth, 94
Ruhleben, 94

Sadler, Sir Michael, 84
Saffron Walden School, 131
St Albans, 52, 54 et seq., 61, 62, 70, 133
St Albans School, 78
Sanitation, 13, 14
Scholl, Sophie, 132
Sculptors in bone, 100
Secondary Modern Schools, 78, 84
Sheffield, city of, 9, 12, 13, 17, 18, 21, 22, 32, 33, 39
Sheffield University, 40
Shop Assistants' Union, 64

Sibford School, 84
Sleaford, 10, 11, 12
Slums, 25, 50, 66
Smallpox, 25
Smith, Copeland, 105, 106
Socialism, 32, 36, 47, 51, 64, 66
Sport, 27, 28
Springfield, Mass., 76
Starvation, 113
Steel industry, 33
Stobs POW camp, 90
Straw-hat industry, 54
Strikes, 36
Sudan War, 45
Sweated industries, 65

Tailoring, in POW camps, 101
Teacher's Pay, 12
Trade unions, 36, 38
Trams, 22
Trevelyan, Sir G. M., 18

Versailles Peace Conference, 114
Verulam, Earl of, 58
Victorian domestic life, 16
Victorian lower middle-class, 11

War, 1914–18, 86 et seq.
Weiss, Charles, 111
Wells, H. G., 64, 130
Welwyn Crafts Guild, 39
Welwyn Garden City, 130, 137, 138
Wheelwright, 22
Willow-growing, in Isle of Man, 104
Winter, John, 43
Wood-carving, 89
Woodworking, 44, 102
World War, 2nd, 133, 137

For Product Safety Concerns and Information please contact our EU
representative GPSR@taylorandfrancis.com
Taylor & Francis Verlag GmbH, Kaufingerstraße 24, 80331 München, Germany

www.ingramcontent.com/pod-product-compliance
Lightning Source LLC
Chambersburg PA
CBHW061451300426
44114CB00014B/1927